THE CHURCH OF GOD IN CHRIST
PRESIDING BISHOP

Bishop J. Drew Sheard

"We've Got Work To Do..."
ST. JOHN 9:4 AND ST. LUKE 10:1-2

Order materials today from the Power for Living Series

Evangelist Terri Hannett • Executive Director
Supervisor Barachias Irons • Chief Editor

Church Of God In Christ
PUBLISHING HOUSE

806 East Brooks Road, Memphis, Tennessee 38116
P. O. Box 161330, Memphis, Tennessee 38186
• **Toll Free:** 1-877-746-8578 | Fax: 901-743-1555
• **Website:** www.cogicpublishinghouse.net
• **Email:** sales@cogicpublishinghouse.net

THE VOICE OF THE PRESIDING BISHOP

Greetings in the Name of our Lord and Savior, Jesus Christ.

As we plan to embark upon a new year, I admonish each of you to take the time to reflect on God's goodness and ask Him to strengthen your hands for the work to be done. Our theme for 2024 is: "We Have Work to Do," John 9:4.

The Chairman of our Publishing Board, Bishop Uleses Henderson, Jr., and the members of that Board have been charged with preparing a curriculum that will challenge your faith and empower you to move forward in the work of the Lord.

I ask that you pray for our church, the leaders, and the congregants of this Grand Ole Church Of God In Christ.

In Ministry,

J. Drew Sheard,

Presiding Bishop and Chief Apostle

Church Of God In Christ, Inc.

THE VOICE OF THE CHAIRMAN OF THE PUBLISHING BOARD

Blessings in the name of the Lord Jesus Christ,

I first want to thank you for your faithful support of our Publishing House. The COVID-19 pandemic presented significant challenges for all of us, but by God's grace, we made it! Now that we are returning to our local churches and Sunday School is reemerging, it is time for us to refocus on equipping God's people with the Word of God.

Our Presiding Bishop reminds us that in 2024, "we've got work to do." Jesus, in John 9:4 (KJV), said, "I must work the works of him that sent me, while it is day: the night cometh, when no man can work." Indeed, 2024 will be the year of produced results. And as we set our hearts and minds to do what God commands us to do, we will see the miraculous hand of God work in our ministries like never before.

It is the job of God's witnesses to carry the Gospel to the far reaches of the world. With the Church Of God In Christ expanding to nearly 120 nations, we aim to share the Word of God with every nation. Your support of the Church Of God In Christ Publishing House enables us to accomplish this mandate.

In Luke 10:2, Jesus told his disciples that "The harvest truly is great, but the labourers are few." Let us be the few because in 2024, we have much work to do!

In His Service,
Bishop Uleses C. Henderson, Jr.
Chairman of the Publishing Board
Church Of God In Christ Inc.

THE VOICE OF MARKETING

From the Chairman of Marketing

Blessings in the name of the Lord,

It is an honor to be counted as a servant of Jesus Christ. There are many honors and titles that we seek after, including those that are bestowed upon us. But the greatest title that we will ever bear witness to is that of servanthood. Being a servant is not easy, but it does require due diligence, it requires faithfulness, and it also requires the ability to die to our wants and desires daily. All of these are constantly working attributes that we, as Christians, should be exuberating throughout the body of Christ. It shows one's ability of the dedication of the heart, the mind, and even the will of a person.

Matthew 9:37-38 AMPC says, "Then He said to His disciples, The harvest is indeed plentiful, but the laborers are few. So, pray to the Lord of the harvest to force out and thrust laborers into His harvest." Working in the field is never easy, but it is rewarding in the fact that we can pour into others to make them better servants. We have an obligation to not just train but to pour into others just like Jesus did and the disciples did. Our Church cannot remain idle and not train the next generation. Therefore, it does not matter about our age, but what matters is that our testimonies, our trials, and our triumphs can keep the Church ready for the next available harvest.

"I must work the works of him that sent me, while it is day: the night cometh, when no man can work"! Let's get to work, everyone.

Mother Sandra S. Jones
Chairman of Marketing
Publishing House

QUARTERLY QUIZ

The questions on this page may be used in several ways: as a pretest at the beginning of the quarter; as a review at the end of the quarter; or as a review after each lesson. The questions are based on the Scripture text of each lesson (King James Version).

LESSON 1

1. Complete **Hebrews 1:9:** "Thou hast loved _____, and hated _____; therefore God, even thy God, hath anointed thee with the _____ of _____ above thy fellows" (KJV).

   _____
   _____

2. The name of the Son is (greater than/less than) the names of others **(Hebrews 1:4).**

   _____
   _____

LESSON 2

1. God is great and above all _____ **(Psalm 95:3).** _____
   _____

2. According to the psalmist, what do the hands of God form **(Psalm 95:4)?** _____
   _____
   _____

LESSON 3

1. How many angels were praising God **(Luke 2:13)?**
   _____
   _____

2. What did the shepherds do after they saw the Savior, the Messiah lying in a manger **(Luke 2:20)?**
   _____
   _____

LESSON 4

1. In **Matthew 14:23,** Jesus sends the people _____, and goes up into the _____ by Himself to _____.
   _____
   _____

2. Why did so many want to see Jesus **(Matthew 14:35)?**
   _____
   _____

LESSON 5

1. How did Jesus tell His disciples to begin their prayer (**Luke 11:2**)?

_____

_____

2. What analogy does Jesus use in **Luke 11:11** to compare God caring for His children?

_____

_____

LESSON 6

1. What does Jesus pray for among believers (**John 17:21**)?

_____

_____

2. Who is Jesus sending into the world as God
sent Him into the world (**John 17:18**)? ____

_____

_____

LESSON 7

1. Who is the great High Priest (**Hebrews 4:14**)? _____

_____

2. Jesus as the High Priest has been called by God after the _____ (**Hebrews 5:10**).

_____

_____

LESSON 8

1. James states that those who are sick should ask for who to respond to their sickness (**James 5:14**)?

_____

_____

2. What were the elders responsibilities do to care for those who are sick (**James 5:14**)?

_____

_____

LESSON 9

1. The king appointed the captive young men to eat and drink what for how many years (**Daniel 1:5**)?

_____

_____

2. Who was concerned for Daniel not following the king's diet? Why (**Daniel 1:10**)?

_____

_____

LESSON 10

1. Who questioned Jesus about inheriting eternal life (**Luke 10:25**)?

_____

_____

2. How did Jesus respond to the question about who is his neighbor (**Luke 10:30**)?

_____

_____

LESSON 11

1. The sheep sit on the _____ _____ of Jesus and the _____ on the _____ (Matthew 25:33).

_____
_____

2. Complete this section of **Matthew 25:35:** Jesus said that when "I was thirsty, and _____ gave _____ _____."

LESSON 12

1. Should believers put on some armor or the whole armor of God (**Ephesians 6:13**)?

_____
_____

2. Paul states that the "feet shod" are for what (**Ephesians 6:15**)?

_____
_____

LESSON 13

1. What did God give to the churches at Macedonia?

_____
_____

2. What lessons can we learn from the generosity of the Saints in Macedonia?

_____
_____

ADULT QUARTERLY

WINTER QUARTER 2024-2025

DECEMBER • JANUARY • FEBRUARY

Unit 1: In Awe of God
DECEMBER

1	Worship Christ's Majesty	9
8	Make A Joyful Noise	15
15	In Awe of Christ's Presence	20
22	Glory To God In The Highest	28
29	A Model For Prayer	36

Unit 2: Learning to Pray
JANUARY

6	Jesus Prays For His Disciples	43
12	Jesus Intercedes For His Disciples	51
19	We Pray For One Another	58
26	Feasting And Fasting	64

Unit 3: Stewardship for Life
FEBRUARY

2	Serving Neighbors, Serving God	71
9	Serving The Least	78
16	Clothed And Ready	85
23	A Community Shares Its Resources	96

LESSON 1 • DECEMBER 1, 2024

WORSHIP CHRIST'S MAJESTY

BIBLE BASIS: HEBREWS 1:1-9

BIBLE TRUTH: Jesus Christ is the gift of salvation that God's people respond to with worship.

MEMORY VERSE: "[Jesus] being the brightness of his glory, and the express image of his person, and upholding all things by the word of his power, when he had by himself purged our sins, sat down on the right hand of the Majesty on high" (Hebrews 1:3).

LESSON AIM: By the end of this lesson, your students will: CONSIDER why Jesus is worthy of adoration and worship; AFFIRM that Jesus' superiority and God's anointing of Him "with the oil of gladness" leads to our response of worship; and lead adults to practice meaningful worship.

BACKGROUND SCRIPTURE: Hebrews 1:1-9; 1 Timothy 1:12-17—Read and incorporate the insights gained from the Background Scriptures into your study of the lesson.

LESSON SCRIPTURE

HEBREWS 1:1-9, KJV

1 God, who at sundry times and in divers manners spake in time past unto the fathers by the prophets,

2 Hath in these last days spoken unto us by his Son, whom he hath appointed heir of all things, by whom also he made the worlds;

3 Who being the brightness of his glory, and the express image of his person, and upholding all things by the word of his power, when he had by himself purged our sins, sat down on the right hand of the Majesty on high:

4 Being made so much better than the angels, as he hath by inheritance obtained a more excellent name than they.

5 For unto which of the angels said he at any time, Thou art my Son, this day have I begotten thee? And again, I will be to him a Father, and he shall be to me a Son?

6 And again, when he bringeth in the firstbegotten into the world, he saith, And let all the angels of God worship him.

7 And of the angels he saith, Who maketh his angels spirits, and his ministers a flame of fire.

8 But unto the Son he saith, Thy throne, O God, is for ever and ever: a sceptre of righteousness is the sceptre of thy kingdom.

9 Thou hast loved righteousness, and hated iniquity; therefore God, even thy God, hath anointed thee with the oil of gladness above thy fellows.

BIBLICAL DEFINITIONS

A. Majesty (Hebrews 1:3) *megalosune* (Gk.)—Greatness; another name for God.

B. Angel (v. 4) *angelos* (Gk.)—Messeger, one who is sent.

LESSON 1 • DECEMBER 1, 2024

LIFE NEED FOR TODAY'S LESSON
AIM: Students will discuss that people praise and honor in various ways.

INTRODUCTION
Instruction to the New Christians Many references to Jewish history are to instruct new Christians. By utilizing language and familiar themes to the audience, the author is instructing and encouraging inexperienced Christians to press towards their new faith. The author contrasts their Jewishness to their Christian identity and explains how being a follower of Christ is similar to and different from Judaism. The author points out that because Christ is superior to figures in their Jewish history, including highly esteemed angels, Jesus is worthy of their faith and worship.

BIBLE LEARNING
AIM: Students will know that Jesus Christ fulfills the three offices of the Hebrew Scriptures—prophet, priest, and king.

I. THE SON OF GOD
(Hebrews 1:1–3)

You will notice that in verses 1–3, the name Jesus is not mentioned; nor the title Christ (Messiah). "Jesus" is not referred to until **Hebrews 2:9**. By not mentioning the name of Jesus Christ until later, the author wishes to grab the readers' attention to the powerful, significance of who Jesus is. This author is not trying to focus all the attention on Jesus' identity merely by highlighting His name, but with the fact that Jesus Christ is God's only begotten Son, and thus God Himself. Jesus' divinity is highlighted.

God's Revelation (verses 1–3)
1 God, who at sundry times and in divers manners spake in time past unto the fathers by the prophets, 2 Hath in these last days spoken unto us by his Son, whom he hath appointed heir of all things, by whom also he made the worlds;

In this epistle, the writer begins with Almighty God because God is the initiator of revelation. The primary focus is on Him, not man. The first and second verses contrast the methods of communication God used in the past with the method He used then. The phrase "at sundry times and in divers manners spake" refers to the fact that God chose the times and methods to communicate. The Old Testament records the clouds, dreams, and visions God used to communicate with His people. God also used the prophets to reveal His Word. The reference to "prophets" here is not limited to the traditional prophets but also includes men of God like Moses, David, and Solomon, to mention a few.

The phrase "in these last days" refers to both the present and end times. There is a clear sense that God has reached the climax of His self-revelation. He has saved the best for last. There is a definite intention to show that this last revelation of God is superior to what He has done in the past. The fact that God has already "spoken unto us by his Son" suggests that, at the time of writing this epistle, the revelation had been completed.

Even though most English translations say "his son" or "the Son," the Greek has no definite article. It simply says "son." Instead of identifying whom God spoke through, it emphasizes the nature of the one whom God spoke through. Unlike the prophets, the Son is much more than a messenger. His divine nature makes Him the right and only capable bearer of God's complete revelation. The rest of Hebrews elaborates on this truth about the identity and the superiority of the revelation of God though JHis Son, Jesus Christ.

The phrase "appointed heir of all things, by whom also he made the worlds" indicates that Christ embodies a dual motif or descriptor of sonship and creation. He is eternal and therefore superior to any other revelation of God. The word translated as "worlds" (**Hebrews 1:2**, KJV) or "universe" (NIV) is *aionas* (Gk. **eye-OWN-as**). It literally means ages or times. The preferred interpretation is "ages," which suggests that Jesus not only created the world but also controls the events of history.

3 Who being the brightness of his glory, and the express image of his person, and upholding all things by the word of his power, when he had by himself purged our sins, sat down on the right hand of the Majesty on high;

In **verse 3**, we get a complete Christology. The first part of the verse talks about the Son's relationship with God, the second part deals with the work of the Son, and the third part refers to His exaltation—the pre-existence, incarnation, and exaltation of Christ. The phrase "brightness of his glory" could mean that Jesus is either the reflection or the radiance of the glory of God. The Bible tells us that God is inapproachable, but that Jesus makes it possible to know Him truly and intimately. What a blessing! The "express image of his person" means "the imprint or seal of God's nature," and the word translated as "person" connotes "the reality or actuality of His being." Thus, Jesus fully represents God (cf. **Colossians 2:9**), and upholds all things by the word of His power. This is not a passive holding up but an active sustaining. Jesus is not only Creator of the universe, but He is also sustaining it by His word. The exaltation of Christ is an allusion to **Psalm 110:1**. Jesus used this verse in silencing the Pharisees concerning his position of Messiah (**Matthew 22:41–46**). The Son of David who is also the pre-incarnate God would come down to earth to die and then be raised to heaven in triumph over all of God's enemies including death. "The Majesty on high" is a title for God. It is a sign of kingship and royal authority.

QUESTIONS 1 & 2
Who has appointed Jesus the heir of all things (**v. 2**)?

How does Jesus sustain all things (**Hebrews 1:3**)?

II. SUPERIOR TO THE ANGELS (vv. 4–9)

In this set of verses, the author continues to build upon the description of Jesus. Let me sketch you a picture, the author seems to say. Imagine the angels. They're pretty important, aren't they? Pretty powerful. Pretty amazing creatures. Well, where do you think Jesus stands in comparison? Higher, the author contends! Jesus is more important, more powerful, and more amazing. than angels.

The Superiority of Christ (verses 4–9)

4 Being made so much better than the angels, as he hath by inheritance obtained a more excellent name than they.

The phrase "better than" or "superior to" is used thirteen times in the Christology presented in Hebrews. Christ is the revelation that is superior to all others. He is the One we are to serve and worship. His revelation

LESSON 1 • DECEMBER 1, 2024

holds more sway in our lives than any other. In the Old Testament, a name (Gk. *onoma*, **AWN-o-maw**) is associated with reputation, and Christ's name/reputation is superior to the angels.

Verse 4 introduces the major subjects of the discussion that is to follow: Christ and the angels. To counter the worship of angels, the writer shows the real position of the angels in contrast to Christ. Remember, Christ is directly related to the Father and the angels are not. Christ inherited the universe and the angels are under His dominion. Christ has a more excellent name due to His pre-existence, incarnation, and exaltation to the right hand of God.

5 For unto which of the angels said he at any time, Thou art my Son, this day have I begotten thee? And again, I will be to him a Father, and he shall be to me a Son?

Hebrews 1:5–14 continues the explanation of who Jesus Christ is, and **Hebrews 2:1–4** challenges the reader to respond appropriately. The author follows this pattern throughout the epistle. He always gives the explanation of who Jesus is and then the challenge to respond appropriately. Beginning with **verse 5**, we find frequent references to, or quotations from, the Old Testament (thirty or more), especially the Psalms. **Verse 5** is a combination of two Old Testament quotations: **Psalm 2:7** and **2 Samuel 7:14**. The truth from **Psalm 2:7** ("Thou art my Son; this day have I begotten thee") concerning Jesus' relationship to God was very significant for the early church's understanding of Christ. This truth was announced from heaven at Jesus' baptism (**Mark 1:10–11**) and preached by Paul (**Acts 13:33–34**). The reference to **2 Samuel 7:14** is taken from the promise to David that he will always have a son to reign on the throne.

This passage carries messianic expectation that the Messiah would be a son of David. The verse in particular shows that not only would the Messiah be a son of David but also a son of God. None of the kings of Israel could claim both of these titles in reality. The only true fulfillment of this was through Christ the son of David and the Son of God.

6 And again, when he bringeth in the firstbegotten into the world, he saith, And let all the angels of God worship him. 7 And of the angels he saith, Who maketh his angels spirits, and his ministers a flame of fire.

The term "first begotten" is translated from the Greek word *prototokos* (**pro-TOE-toe-kose**). It does not mean the first to be created. Rather, it indicates privilege, authority, and inheritance. Its meaning centers on the firstborn son's rights and position. Christ has the highest authority. The phrase "all the angels of God worship him" emphasizes His exalted state as God because only God can be worshiped. Since the angels worship Him, do not worship the angels. Worship Christ! This seals the exaltation of Christ over the angels. Even the angels know that He is superior, and therefore they bow down and worship Him. This is not an exaltation of His human nature but the recognition of who He truly is as the Son of God.

Verse 7 contains an Old Testament quotation from **Psalm 104:4**. It further shows the superiority of Christ over angels. They not only worship Him, but serve Him. **Psalm 104:4** is taken from a passage about creation. While Christ created the world, the angels were just instruments in the overall act of creation. They are servants and agents of God in creating the world. The angels are subordinate to Christ. They are spirits and flames of fire. This suggests their temporality and

LESSON 1 • DECEMBER 1, 2024

transient nature. This is placed in contrast to the eternality of the Son.

8 But unto the Son he saith, Thy throne, O God, is for ever and ever: a sceptre of righteousness is the sceptre of thy kingdom. 9 Thou hast loved righteousness, and hated iniquity; therefore God, even thy God, hath anointed thee with the oil of gladness above thy fellows.

These verses are a quotation of **Psalm 45:6–7. Psalm 45** is a marriage psalm calling a princess to heed the king's call and "forget also thine own people and thy father's house" (**v. 10**) in order to enter the king's palace, where there is great joy. This king loves righteousness and hates sin. This psalm has many messianic applications. **Hebrews 1:8–9** refers to the Son as God and says that His throne is exalted forever. Christ is superior to the angels—"anointed with the oil of gladness above thy fellows."

BIBLE APPLICATION

AIM: Students will acknowledge that Jesus is God's Son.

People in society often esteem other people. Presidents, kings, queens, athletes, and celebrities receive praise for their status and achievements. When President Barack Obama was elected, for example, many thought he would take the "presidential throne" as a type of savior. During the challenging civil rights era of the fifties and sixties, many Americans looked up to Dr. Martin Luther King Jr. as a drum major for justice and savior.

But today's passage draws our attention to the one who is most deserving of all our praise and worship: Jesus, God's Son. How often do we find ourselves worshiping Him instead of finding ourselves at the feet of a person in society?

STUDENTS' RESPONSES

AIM: Students will acknowledge that they have a deep desire to worship God.

Sometimes when we read the Bible, it is tempting to view Jesus as a man. Even Christians can forget the significance of Jesus being God. How can you shape your worship of Jesus to start with the fact that He is God instead of what He's done for you?

PRAYER

God, our Father, we thank you for giving us Jesus. For Jesus is higher than the angels and us. He is superior to all people and anything that has or will be created or made. We worship and adore You for allowing us to have fellowship with Jesus, our Redeemer, and our Savior. In Jesus' Name we pray. Amen.

DIG A LITTLE DEEPER
Worship Christ's Majesty

Hebrews 1:1-9 opens with a profound declaration of the majesty of Christ. Just look how the text begins by emphasizing how God, in the past, spoke to humanity through various prophets, but in these last days, He has chosen to communicate through His Son, Jesus Christ. God is establishing the superiority of Christ's revelation over all previous messages.

The passage then probes the majestic attributes of Christ. Make no mistake: He is described as the "heir of all things," signifying His divine inheritance and authority over the entire universe. Now, Christ is identified as the one through whom God created the world, emphasizing His role in the act of creation itself.

His radiance and the exact representation of God's nature showcase His divine identity. The sustaining power of Christ is highlighted as He upholds all things by His word, underscoring His omnipotence. The pas-

LESSON 1 • DECEMBER 1, 2024

sage also emphasizes His redemptive work, noting how He made purification for sins, highlighting His role as the ultimate High Priest who offered Himself as a perfect sacrifice for humanity's salvation.

If you ever questioned Christ's position to the angels, please note that He is superior to them due to His unique identity and divine authority and worthy of total worship. To conclude, Hebrews 1:1-9 paints a majestic portrait of Christ as the divine Son of God, the Creator, Sustainer, Redeemer, and the ultimate source of divine revelation, deserving of our worship and adoration.

HOW TO SAY IT

Superior. Soo-**PEE**-ri-or.

Subordinate. Su-**BOR**-din-it.

Allusion. Uh-**LOO**-shin.

DAILY HOME BIBLE READINGS

MONDAY
Great and Awesome God
(Daniel 9:3–10)

TUESDAY
O Lord, Hear and Forgive
(Daniel 9:11–19)

WEDNESDAY
God the Almighty Reigns
(Revelation 19:1–8)

THURSDAY
First and Last, Beginning and End
(Revelation 22:8–14)

FRIDAY
My Son, the Beloved
(Matthew 3:13–17)

SATURDAY
Honor and Glory Forever

(1 Timothy 1:12–17)

SUNDAY
The Son Reflects God's Glory
(Hebrews 1:1–9)

PREPARE FOR NEXT SUNDAY

Read **Psalm 95:1–7a** and study "Make a Joyful Noise."

Sources:
Hamilton, Victor P. *Handbook on the Pentateuch: Genesis, Exodus, Leviticus, Numbers, Deuteronomy.* Grand Rapids, MI: Baker Academic, 2005.
Keener, Craig S. *The IVP Bible Background Commentary.* Downers Grove, IL: Intervarsity Press, 1993

COMMENTS / NOTES:

LESSON 2 • DECEMBER 8, 2024

MAKE A JOYFUL NOISE

BIBLE BASIS: PSALM 95:1–7a

BIBLE TRUTH: God is the rock of our salvation and is worthy of praise and worship.

MEMORY VERSE: "O come, let us sing unto the LORD: let us make a joyful noise to the rock of our salvation" (Psalm 95:1).

LESSON AIM: By the end of the lesson, your students will: DISCERN that God is the Creator of the earth and the maker of humankind, and God is truly worthy of praise; EXPERIENCE the enthusiasm, power, and excitement that comes when believers praise God as their divine King; and SHED inhibitions in worship and praise God exuberantly.

BACKGROUND SCRIPTURE: Psalm 95:1–7a; 1 Timothy 1:12–17—Read and incorporate the insights gained from the Background Scriptures into your study of the lesson.

LESSON SCRIPTURE

PSALM 95:1–7A, KJV

1 O come, let us sing unto the LORD: let us make a joyful noise to the rock of our salvation.

2 Let us come before his presence with thanksgiving, and make a joyful noise unto him with psalms.

3 For the LORD is a great God, and a great King above all gods.

4 In his hand are the deep places of the earth: the strength of the hills is his also.

5 The sea is his, and he made it: and his hands formed the dry land.

6 O come, let us worship and bow down: let us kneel before the LORD our maker.

7a For he is our God; and we are the people of his pasture, and the sheep of his hand.

BIBLICAL DEFINITIONS

A. Psalms (Psalm 95:2) *zemir* (Heb.)—an instrumental song; a song with words accompanied by musical instruments. The beauty of musical instruments as a part of worship was greatly developed by King David.

B. Thanksgiving (v. 2) *todah* (Heb.)—adoration, praise. Appears approximately 30 times in the Old Testament, a dozen of these in the Psalms.

LIFE NEED FOR TODAY'S LESSON

AIM: Students will understand that many people realize that a power beyond them gives meaning to their lives.

INTRODUCTION

An Invitation to Worship

Psalm 95 is an invitation to worship. Perhaps the psalmist is pushing the crowd or congregation who had grown weary. It seemed that they'd stopped believing, and were no longing expecting God to fulfill His promises. The author, tired of their passivity,

LESSON 2 • DECEMBER 8, 2024

essentially said, "Don't just stand there; do something!" Through the psalm, the psalmist exhorted the people to serve God.

One cannot worship God with a hardened heart, as this psalm warns. In **verse 8**, the psalmist used the testing at Meribah (also known as Massah) as an example. At Meribah, the Israelites sinned against God (**Exodus 17:1-7**). "Is the Lord among us or not?" they complained. Not trusting God in the wilderness kept them out of the Promised Land. In our text, the psalmist admonished the congregation to not let the same happen to them. "Come, let us sing to the one who'll save us," he urged. The same testing is referenced in **Hebrews 3:7** and **4:7** as a warning to believers.

BIBLE LEARNING

AIM: Students will learn that in Psalms, calls to worship were often hymns sung by the ancient community.

I. PRAISE HIM (Psalm 95:1–2)

Praising God was as natural to the psalmist as breathing. Psalms is full of praises, adoration, and worship to God. Even when things were bad, the psalmist poured out his heart to the Rock of his salvation. The "Rock" is a recurrent metaphor for God in Psalms, used over 20 times.

The psalmist sees the worship of God as something to be done corporately. He exhorts the congregation with the words "Come, let us sing together." It is an invitation to praise the Rock of our salvation, but at the same time the psalmist is also leading the way by including himself in the invitation. He says "us" so that the call is personal as well as corporate.

Joyful Thanksgiving (verses 1–2)

1 O come, let us sing unto the LORD: let us make a joyful noise to the rock of our salvation. 2 Let us come before his presence with thanksgiving, and make a joyful noise unto him with psalms.

The psalm begins the call to worship with an imperative (come), followed by four verbs exhorting the people to sing and rejoice in God's presence. It is more than an invitation to worship the Lord, the Rock our salvation; it is a powerful summons to worship God with a joy that compels His people to shout. The psalmist is filled with such jubilation at God's power that words are not enough. Music is necessary to express such awe and adoration.

The people are urged to enter God's presence. In the Old Testament, God's presence is described as His very face. God is not just a transcendent Creator and Ruler who is not involved personally with His creation. God interacts face-to-face with those who worship Him, and since their worship brings them faceto-face with their Creator, they must sing!

QUESTION 1

How should we come into His presence (**Isaiah 53:2**)?

II. ADORE HIM (vv. 3–5)

As if the people had asked why they should praise the Lord, the psalmist answered. "Because He is great." Then, he gave evidence of God's greatness by recalling that He held the deep places of the earth in His hand. Essentially he challenged, "If things that are out of sight and out of reach are in His hands, how much more so are your problems?"

LESSON 2 • DECEMBER 8, 2024

A Great God (verses 3–5)

3 For the LORD is a great God, and a great King above all gods.

The psalm begins the explanation of the reasons for worshiping God. Not only is the Lord a great God, but He is also greater than all other gods. In antiquity, the Israelites always had neighbors who worshiped other gods, and the Old Testament narrates many times when the Israelites were tempted to, and sometimes did, worship those false deities. Here the psalm contains a metaphor the people would comprehend because they were ruled by kings and understood the authority and power that a king had. Just as David, Solomon, and the other Israelite kings had authority and power over the people, so the Lord has authority and power over all gods. For anyone tempted to worship other gods, this psalm reminds them that their God is the one with power over everything.

4 In his hand are the deep places of the earth: the strength of the hills is his also. 5 The sea is his, and he made it: and his hands formed the dry land.

God is the Creator of all things. The deep places and the hills represent creation from top to bottom. Similarly, **v. 5** mentions water and dry land. These opposite pictures of the depths and the hills, as well as water and dry land, form an all-encompassing picture of God's creation. In addition, the reference to the sea and the dry land echoes the Exodus, reminding the people of the miraculous ways in which God saves those of faith. Bookending these verses with God's hands also creates an image of His hands encompassing all of creation. God created everything and cares for everything.

In the Old Testament, God's hand represents not only the things He touches and tends to, but also His power and strength. Literally, God's hand touches all parts of the earth, including the heights of the mountains. Metaphorically, God's power and strength as Creator are reflected in the very foundations and heights of creation. God's hand is both powerful and caring, and tends to all of His creation.

III. WORSHIP HIM (vv. 6–7)

The psalmist recognized pride can hinder our relationship with God. The antidote to pridefulness is worship. By showing God how much He is worth to us, we realize our true worth in relationship to Him. This is a surefire cure for pride: "Bow down and worship the Lord who made us." **Psalm 100:3** also points to God as our Creator, saying, "... it is he that hath made us, and not we ourselves."

Bow Before the Lord (verses 6–7a)

6 O come, let us worship and bow down: let us kneel before the LORD our maker.

Parallel to **verse 1** in structure, this verse once again commands the people to worship God, adding new forms of worship to the noisy singing and rejoicing of **vv. 1–2**. Although the first exhortative verb, *shachah* (Heb. **shah-KHAH**), is translated "worship," it also means to bow down because it carries the connotation of submitting to someone in authority. As a result, all three verbs describing worship in this verse indicate physical bowing before God the Creator. The final verb for kneeling, *barak* (Heb. **bah-RAHK**), can also indicate blessing in other contexts where God blesses the faithful, establishing a relationship between God

LESSON 2 • DECEMBER 8, 2024

as the one who blesses and the people as worshipers. In addition, the epithet for God as our Maker reminds the people that God has created not only the earth and the sea but also the people, and they should worship Him by surrendering 100 percent to Him.

7a For he is our God; and we are the people of his pasture, and the sheep of his hand.

Similar to **v. 3**, **7a** explains why the people should worship with submission. Quite simply, the Lord is our God. The metaphor shifts from God as Creator to God as Shepherd. Now God's hand of care and power is involved in tending to His flock. The remainder of the psalm carries out this metaphor by reminding the people that their ancestors did not always follow God, even though they knew about His works. Amid a psalm of praise and worship, the final verses serve as a reminder of the need for such psalms. Even God's faithful can forget how to worship God, so the psalm calls the people to keep worshiping God with song and submission lest they too forget His power and mighty deeds.

QUESTION 2

What is the posture for worship (**v. 6**)?

BIBLE APPLICATION

AIM: Students will worship God as the Creator of heaven and earth.

Our society promotes pridefulness, often concealing it as self-confidence. Bestseller lists tout titles that reveal seven or ten steps to self-promotion. The Bible shows us that promotion comes from the Lord (**Psalm 75:6**). Our text reminds us that one must come before the Lord humbly and with thanksgiving—certainly not positions of pride, especially while on bended knee.

STUDENTS' RESPONSES

AIM: Students will learn to shed inhibitions in worship and praise God exuberantly.

This week, practice joyfulness. No matter how challenging your days get, sing songs of praise to God. Remember that you belong to God, not the other way around. Instead of standing, complaining, and prolonging your pain, get on your knees and worship. Bow down and thank Him for the things that are good and right.

PRAYER

Lord, we praise You with great thanksgiving. We worship You in reverence and with great anticipation of Your marvelous acts in all of creation. In Jesus' Name we pray. Amen.

DIG A LITTLE DEEPER
Make a Joyful Noise

Integral to our lives as believers' is the understanding of the power of praise and worship. This psalm reminds us that our worship should be filled with exuberance and joy because we serve a God who is worthy. We are encouraged to shout for joy and worship the Lord with gladness. Praise does not have to be cute or pretty, nor follow specific denominational guidelines. It is not a style, specific dance, or specific noise.

The foundational truth for us as believers is that we know that the Lord is God. We believe in the one true God who created us and sustains us. In acknowledging His lordship in our lives, we proclaim that He is so worthy of our praise. Our founder, Bishop Charles H. Mason, would always be heard saying, 'Be glad about Him'. We worship with joy and gladness because it recognizes the greatness of our God.

LESSON 2 • DECEMBER 8, 2024

'When you have a personal relationship with God, your praise should not be defined by others but should spring from your heart. Praise is necessary for us because it is our expression of admiration, gratitude, reverence, and devotion offered to Him in acknowledgment of His greatness, goodness, and sovereignty. We seldom give God all the credit that He deserves, but sincere praise is a beginning. It is not a process but an expression. Too often, praise is reduced to our emotions. Therefore, there are two times to praise the Lord: Praise Him when you feel like it and praise Him when you don't.

HOW TO SAY IT

Exhortation. eks-or-**TAY**-shun.

Transcendent. tran-**SEN**-dent.

DAILY HOME BIBLE READINGS

MONDAY
Hold Fast to God
(Deuteronomy 13:1–8)

TUESDAY
Devote Yourselves to the Lord (1 Kings 8:54–62)

WEDNESDAY
Worship with Reverence and Awe
(Hebrews 12:22–29)

THURSDAY
Sing Praises to God

(1 Chronicles 16:7–15)

FRIDAY
Ascribe Greatness to Our God
(Deuteronomy 32:1–7)

SATURDAY
A Sacrifice of Praise to God
(Hebrews 13:6–15)

SUNDAY
Let Us Worship and Bow Down
(Psalm 95:1–7a)

PREPARE FOR NEXT SUNDAY

Read **Matthew 14:22-36** and study *"In Awe of Christ's Presence."*

Sources:
Bellinger, W. H. *Psalms: Reading and Studying the Book of Praises.* Peabody, MA: Hendrickson Publishers, 1990.
Mays, James Luther. *Psalms. Interpretation: A Bible Commentary for Teaching and Preaching.* Edited by James Luther Mays, Patrick D. Miller, Jr. and
Paul J. Achtemeier. Louisville, KY: Westminster John Knox Press, 1994. McCann, J. Clinton, Jr. "The Book of Psalms." *Vol. IV of The New Interpreter's
Bible.* 12 vols. Edited by Leander E. Keck, et al. Nashville, TN: Abingdon Press, 1996. 641–1280.
The Word in Life Study Bible. Nashville, TN: Thomas Nelson, 1993. 149.
The New Spirit Filled Life Bible. Nashville, TN: Thomas Nelson, 2002. 687–688, 760.

LESSON 3 • DECEMBER 15, 2024

IN AWE OF CHRIST'S PRESENCE

BIBLE BASIS: MATTHEW 14:22–36

BIBLE TRUTH: Matthew tells about the times when Jesus miraculously walked on water to meet his disciples in a boat, which led them to worship him as truly the Son of God, and when Jesus healed the sick.

MEMORY VERSE: "And when they were come into the ship, the wind ceased. Then they that were in the ship came and worshipped him, saying, Of a truth thou art the Son of God" (Matthew 14:32–33).

LESSON AIM: By the end of the lesson, your students will: REVIEW the disciples' response to Jesus' miracles; be INSPIRED by the miracles of Jesus and YEARN to become faithful worshipers; and BELIEVE in Jesus' miracles and commit to being prayerful encouragers of others.

BACKGROUND SCRIPTURE: LUKE 2; Psalm 19—Read and incorporate the insights gained from the Background Scriptures into your study of the lesson.

LESSON SCRIPTURE

MATTHEW 14:22–36, KJV

22 And straightway Jesus constrained his disciples to get into a ship, and to go before him unto the other side, while he sent the multitudes away.

23 And when he had sent the multitudes away, he went up into a mountain apart to pray: and when the evening was come, he was there alone.

24 But the ship was now in the midst of the sea, tossed with waves: for the wind was contrary.

25 And in the fourth watch of the night Jesus went unto them, walking on the sea.

26 And when the disciples saw him walking on the sea, they were troubled, saying, It is a spirit; and they cried out for fear.

27 But straightway Jesus spake unto them, saying, Be of good cheer; it is I; be not afraid.

28 And Peter answered him and said, Lord, if it be thou, bid me come unto thee on the water.

29 And he said, Come. And when Peter was come down out of the ship, he walked on the water, to go to Jesus.

30 But when he saw the wind boisterous, he was afraid; and beginning to sink, he cried, saying, Lord, save me.

31 And immediately Jesus stretched forth his hand, and caught him, and said unto him, O thou of little faith, wherefore didst thou doubt?

32 And when they were come into the ship, the wind ceased.

33 Then they that were in the ship came and worshipped him, saying, Of a truth thou art the Son of God.

34 And when they were gone over, they came into the land of Gennesaret.

35 And when the men of that place had knowledge of him, they sent out into all that country round about, and brought unto him all that were diseased;

LESSON 3 • DECEMBER 15, 2024

36 And besought him that they might only touch the hem of his garment: and as many as touched were made perfectly whole.

BIBLICAL DEFINITIONS

A. Joy (Luke 2:10) *chara* (Gk.)— Gladness, happiness; or the cause or object of such.
B. Messiah (v. 11) *Christos* (Gk.) Christ, the Anointed One.

LIFE NEED FOR TODAY'S LESSON

AIM: Students will learn that many things inspire awe in people.

INTRODUCTION
His Unquestionable Power

It greatly troubled Jesus dealing with the devastating news of the imprisonment and execution of his cousin, John the Baptist, at the hands of Herod the tetrarch (**Matthew 14:1–13**). He needed to get away from the crowd to retreat by Himself to a remote place to rest. But crowds of people from surrounding towns began to seek after Jesus. As the evening set in, the disciples tried to send the people to fend for themselves for dinner, but Jesus objected. He ordered His disciples to give the people something to eat. The disciples were perplexed at Jesus' command, but it was all a setup for a display of His unquestionable power and convincing proof of His ability to defy natural law. With five loaves and two fishes, Jesus blessed His Father and turned little into overflow, feeding five thousand men, not including women and children (**Matthew 14:13–21**). After this, Jesus sent the disciples away by boat to the other side of the Sea of Galilee while He recharged in prayer.

BIBLE LEARNING

AIM: Students will know Jesus' miracles are evidence of His divinity.

I. JESUS REPLENISHES HIS POWER (Matthew 14:22–23)

Jesus, after His exhausting time of ministry and meeting the spiritual and natural needs of the people, again tries to commune alone with His Father in prayer. Jesus sends the disciples ahead of Him by boat while dismissing the crowds that gathered to see Him. He needed to be alone with His Father to recharge and regroup.

Time to Leave (verses 22–23)

22 And straightway Jesus constrained his disciples to get into a ship, and to go before him unto the other side, while he sent the multitudes away.

Jesus multiplied bread for five thousand people in a desert place (**vv. 13–21**) where He had retreated with His disciples. His withdrawal was motivated by a report of Herod's beheading of His cousin John the Baptist and by the king's comments about Him and the miracles He was performing (**vv. 1–2, 13**). After feeding the people with the bread, they were overwhelmed and wanted to appoint Him king (**John 6:15**). Jesus rejected this as a potential threat to His mission on earth. Jesus' purpose on earth was to serve, not to be served (**Matthew 20:28; Mark 10:45**, NLT).

This situation led Jesus to constrain His disciples to leave the scene immediately while He dismissed the crowd. The Greek word for constrained is *anagkazo* (**aw-nawng-KADzo**) which means to physically or mentally compel or force somebody to do something. It is derived from *anagke* (Gk. **aw-NAWNG-kay**), which means necessity or need. There was an imperative motive for Jesus to send His disciples ahead. Carson states that Jesus wanted to "tame a messianic uproar" (Matthew, 343).

The disciples had to go to "the other side," which according to scholars refers to the western side of the Sea of Galilee. However, the synoptic parallel in Mark adds "to Bethsaida" (**6:45**), where **Luke 9:10** also locates the feeding of the five thousand. Some scholars suggest that the desert place where the feeding took place was closer but separated from Bethsaida by a bay. Jesus intended the disciples to wait for Him at Bethsaida, but the contrary wind took them to Gennesaret. A similar situation happened in **Acts 27:15**, where the boat driving Paul and the other crew members was carried away from its initial course by a strong wind.

23 And when he had sent the multitudes away, he went up into a mountain apart to pray: and when the evening was come, he was there alone.

After He has sent them away, He climbed the mountain to communicate with the Father. At some critical periods of Jesus' earthly ministry, He isolated Himself from the crowd and even His disciples to pray. **Luke 5:16** explains that Jesus was withdrawing in the wilderness for prayer in periods of great popularity. In **Matthew 6:6**, Jesus urgently asks us to withdraw in our closet to pray to God. It is important for us Christians today to emulate our Lord and retreat ourselves from noise and busyness at times to pray. He was alone at evening. We should not be confused about the use of "evening" twice in this chapter in the narrative sequence. The Jews divided the day into three periods: morning, noon, and evening (cf. **Psalm 55:17**). The evening was in turn subdivided into two parts: the first evening began at sunset (twilight) and the second began when the sun was fully set (dusk) (cf. **Exodus 12:6**, literally "between the evenings"). The Greek word for evening was *opsios* (**OP-see-os**) which could refer either to the period before sunset or right after sundown, but was sometimes used for the two. In context, however, it is logical to ascribe the first mention of evening (**14:15**) to the first evening and the current one after sunset. Jesus was left praying alone when it was night.

II. JESUS DEFIES THE LAWS OF NATURE (vv. 24–27)

Matthew shifts the scene. While on the boat, the disciples encounter torrential winds and waves in their travel, which is very unsettling even for the trade fishermen to navigate. In this brewing storm, between 3 and 6 o'clock in the morning, the disciples see a figure walking toward them and become terrified. Out of fear, their imaginations take them to the worst possible scenario, and they conclude that it was a threatening figure. They begin to scream out with terror, "It's a ghost!" not realizing that it was Jesus (**v. 26**, NLT). Upon their reaction, Jesus immediately calls on His disciples to calm down and "take courage" (**v. 27**, NLT) because He has arrived on the scene among the waves and wind.

The Strength of Contrary Winds (verses 24–27)

24 But the ship was now in the midst of the sea, tossed with waves: for the wind was contrary.

While Jesus was on the mountain praying, the disciples were on the sea tossed with waves. They encountered a contrary wind that would eventually lead them to Gennesaret. **Mark 6:48** tells us that Jesus saw that the disciples were battling with the contrary wind. We cannot be certain if Jesus saw them physically or supernaturally. The current event is taking place after they had left the desert place for quite a long time. Still, John states that it was already night when they encountered the wind. It would have been difficult for Jesus to see from such a long distance. Some suggest that it was the full moon and Jesus could see from the mountain. In any case, if Jesus in the beginning of His ministry could see Nathanael (**John 1:50**) from afar, it is not unlikely that He could see the disciples by the divine endowments of the Holy Spirit.

25 And in the fourth watch of the night Jesus went unto them, walking on the sea.

The Jews divided the night into three watches and the Romans divided it into four between 6 p.m. and 6 a.m. Jesus therefore came to the disciples between three and six o'clock in the morning. Around this time, Jesus appeared to them in an unprecedented fashion by walking on the sea. Great figures of Old Testament history such as Moses, Joshua, Elijah, and Elisha did miracles involving parting of water bodies, but never has it been recorded that anyone walked on water (**Exodus 14:21, 22; Joshua 3:15–17; 2 Kings 2:8, 14**). This action of Jesus clearly portrays His divine nature. There was probably no boat left for Him to join the disciples.

26 And when the disciples saw him walking on the sea, they were troubled, saying, It is a spirit; and they cried out for fear.

The disciples saw someone walking on water at night and with a contrary wind. The disciples could not fathom this scene, assuming the being they saw was a spirit. The Greek word for spirit here is *phantasma* (**FAN-tas-mah**), meaning phantom or "a ghost" (NLT). Our perception of reality always shapes our responses and reactions. They expressed their inner feelings of fear outwardly by a strident noise. Their fear could have been due to prevailing cultural beliefs of the time. In the ancient Near East, the sea was thought to be the realm of powerful, chaotic beings (cf. **Job 41; Revelation 13:1**). They undoubtedly thought Jesus was a "ghost" that would do them harm. Their deduction that it was a ghost led them to fear, *phobos* (**FOBos**), which means fear, dread, terror—that which is caused by intimidation or adversaries. Hagner compares the "fear of the disciples" to that of "all who are threatened by insecurity in the face of the unknown" (425).

27 But straightway Jesus spake unto them, saying, be of good cheer; it is I; be not afraid.

The Lord is always prompt in coming to rescue us. "Be of good cheer" or "do not be afraid" (NLT) are phrases of encouragement and comfort. It resonates when we have a challenging task ahead; it will re-echo if we are in peril or in the face of danger, such as the current case facing the disciples.

The Lord wants us to "be of good cheer" and not be afraid because of His presence. "It is I" is the translation of *ego eimi* (Gk. **eg-O ay-MEE**), which echoes the "I am" God's self-revelation to Moses in **Exodus 3:14** and other similar passages like **Isaiah 43:12**. We have this promise of Jesus in **Matthew 28:20**: "I am with you always, even to the end of the age" (NLT). We

LESSON 3 • DECEMBER 15, 2024

should therefore not be afraid even in our darkest circumstances or the most violent storm of our lives.

III. JESUS CALLS PETER TO STEP OUT (vv. 28–29)

Peter, being often the spokesman of the group and bold enough to ask the tough questions, puts Jesus to the test after hearing His voice. Peter responds, "Lord, if it's really you, tell me to come to you, walking on the water" (**v. 28**, NLT). It was Peter's personality to take Jesus at His word and take risks of faith which would prove to be invaluable for his future role in the church.

Peter's Faith (verses 28–29)

28 And Peter answered him and said, Lord, if it be thou, bid me come unto thee on the water.

Peter's request was not portraying a doubt about the identity of the one walking on water. Carson suggests the phrase "since it is you" is an acceptable rendering of "if it be thou." Peter is an extrovert as far as personality is concerned. His request might have been guided by the delegation of power Jesus granted them in **Mark 6:12, 13, 30** over sicknesses and demons. Since it was the Lord, He can grant Peter with this authority over physical laws also.

29 And he said, Come. And when Peter was come down out of the ship, he walked on the water, to go to Jesus.

Jesus granted Peter's request by the word "come." It should not be perceived here as a mere invitation but rather as a delegation of power or a transfer of authority. Peter therefore took the first step and came out of the ship. Once he was out of the boat and on the sea, he could walk just as Jesus was doing. **John 14:12** says that "anyone who believes in me will do the same works I have done..." (NLT).

QUESTION 1
What was Peter's response to the sight of Jesus walking on water (**Matthew 14:28**)?

IV. JESUS' POWER DECLARED (vv. 30–36)

We can only imagine what the other disciples were thinking as Peter launched out into the deep. As he continued, he began to notice within his natural senses what was happening around him and became afraid. The wind got stronger, and as it pressed his body, he began to get nervous, which caused him to take his eyes off Jesus. Again, how often do we take our eyes off Jesus when things don't look like what we expect, even though we have been given a word from the Lord to go forward in faith?

Peter's Fear (verses 30–36)

30 But when he saw the wind boisterous, he was afraid; and beginning to sink, he cried, saying, Lord, save me.

We can perform greater works by faith as long as we keep on looking at the Lord who instructs us. Anytime we shift our focus from the Lord to the challenge, we will start to experience failure. Here Peter fails to look at the Lord, who instructed him to come, but rather focused on the wind.

When Peter realized he was sinking, he cried to Jesus, saying, "Lord save me." Our faith may fail us at times, but ultimately Jesus is our last recourse in peril or danger. Instinctively, Peter cried out of fear and despair for the rescue of the Lord.

LESSON 3 • DECEMBER 15, 2024

31 And immediately Jesus stretched forth his hand, and caught him, and said unto him, O thou of little faith, wherefore didst thou doubt?

Jesus did not tarry in rescuing Peter. Without any delay, He stretched His hand to seize the drowning Peter. Peter walked quite a distance since Jesus could just stretch His hand to get hold of Him.

Jesus rebuked him after He got hold of him. The Greek word for "little faith" is *oligopistos* (**o-lee-GO-pis-tos**), and it is used only by the Lord to gently rebuke His disciples for their anxiety. Our cry of desperation will always be heard, and God will swiftly deliver us from our trouble, but we must expect a gentle rebuke from our loving Lord. This word suggests a quantification of faith just as Jesus explained the amount of faith required to move mountains in **Matthew 17:20**.

32 And when they were come into the ship, the wind ceased.

This verse indicates that Peter walked back with Jesus into the boat. When they (Jesus and Peter) entered the ship, the wind ceased.

33 Then they that were in the ship came and worshipped him, saying, of a truth thou art the Son of God.

When the wind ceased, the disciples realized the true personality of Jesus. This man could multiply five loaves of bread for five thousand people, walk on water, and still the wind. Who could that person be except the promised Son of God? The Roman officer and the soldiers made the same confession when they witnessed the events at Jesus' death and were filled with awe (**Matthew 27:50–54**).

The term used for worship is *proskunein* (**pros-KOO-nayn**), which signifies to fall prostrate in front of the one being worshiped. The same word is used when Cornelius welcomed Peter into his house. Peter's objection that he was also a man points to the fact that the term is used only for divine being (**Acts 10:25–26**).

34 And when they were gone over, they came into the land of Gennesaret.

After crossing the lake, they landed at Gennesaret, described as a triangular coastal land on the western side of the lake.

35 And when the men of that place had knowledge of him, they sent out into all that country round about, and brought unto him all that were diseased;

Jesus was already very famous and He could not move unnoticed. John even records that the people who were fed the previous day went after Jesus to the other side of the lake (**John 6:24–25**). The people of that area spread the news about Jesus' arrival in their territory, and they brought sick people to Jesus for healing. The term used to describe the sick people could mean physical or mental illness (Gk. *kakos*, **kaw-KOSE**).

36 And besought him that they might only touch the hem of his garment: and as many as touched were made perfectly whole.

The hem of His garments probably refers to the fringes or tassel at the corner of Christ's mantle; it was a Jewish religious requirement in **Numbers 15:37–39** and **Deuteronomy 22:12**. The request to only touch the fringe of the garments might be due to the crowds at the place. Anyone who was able to touch Him was made perfectly whole, meaning a complete restoration, similar to the woman with the blood issue (**Luke 8:44, 48**).

LESSON 3 • DECEMBER 15, 2024

QUESTION 2

How did Jesus react to the disciples and Peter's trouble on the water (**vv. 27, 31**)?

BIBLE APPLICATION

AIM: Students will be inspired by the miracles of Jesus and yearn to become faithful worshipers.

God is still performing signs and wonders today as we call on the name of His Son Jesus. We should seek the Lord's will for our lives to receive vision and be empowered by the Holy Spirit to get in alignment to make the miraculous happen in our age. The same power that raised Jesus from the dead lives within us. Just as the apostles turned the world upside down at the word of the Lord to establish the church, we live on as His fruit on the earth.

STUDENTS' RESPONSES

AIM: Students will be comforted and encouraged by Jesus.

We are encouraged to fix our eyes on Jesus, the Author and Finisher of our faith, who for the sake of the joy set before Him endured the Cross and is seated at the right hand of the throne of God (**Hebrews 12:2**). If we truly believe that Jesus ever lives to make intercession for us, we must trust that we are safe in His arms and follow His lead.

PRAYER

Jesus, thank You for providing for us and protecting us. You are truly a loving and forgiving Savior. In Jesus' Name we pray. Amen.

DIG A LITTLE DEEPER
Glory to God in the Highest

Bethlehem, at the time of Jesus' birth, was a place of profound significance and activity. Multiple events converged in preparation for the arrival of the Messiah. While tending to their flocks, shepherds witnessed divine interventions with angels making momentous announcements, followed by an angelic chorus singing songs of praise. Meanwhile, the virgin mother, Mary, was ready to give birth, and Joseph stood by as the earthly father. Unbeknownst to many, Jews from all corners gathered for a census, oblivious to the fulfillment of ancient messianic prophecies. The birth's location and circumstances defied the people's expectations of a grandiose arrival for the King of Kings, yet this was God's meticulously orchestrated plan.

This passage lies at the core of Christian belief, shaping our understanding of Christ's birth, His divine nature, purpose, and the impact on those who encounter Him. It prompts reflection on how many, even amidst these extraordinary events, missed the fulfillment of prophecy. Doubt, fear, social status, or sheer ignorance may have blinded them. Some were perhaps so absorbed in their own lives that they missed this pivotal moment.

Like many today, we often rush through the holidays, preoccupied with earthly rituals, parties, programs, and gifts, sidelining the true significance of Christmas. Have we become so ensnared in secularism and commercialism that we disregard the real essence of this season? The greatest gift has arrived—the long-awaited Savior, Christ the Lord. God's message is accessible to all; Jesus still embodies good news for everyone, exceeding social, economic, and worldly distinctions.

LESSON 3 • DECEMBER 15, 2024

HOW TO SAY IT

Gennesaret. juh-**NES**-uh-ret.

Galilee. **GAL**-uh-lee.

Bethsaida. beth-**SAY**-uh-duh.

DAILY HOME BIBLE READINGS

MONDAY
By Faith We Please God
(Hebrews 11:1–6)

TUESDAY
Where is Your Faith?
(Luke 8:19–25)

WEDNESDAY
I Believe; Help My Unbelief
(Mark 9:15–24)

THURSDAY
The Light Overpowers Darkness
(John 1:1–9)

FRIDAY
A Mustard-Seed-Sized Faith
(Matthew 17:14–20)

SATURDAY
Great is Your Faith
(Matthew 15:21–31)

SUNDAY
Oh, You of Little Faith
(Matthew 14:22–36)

PREPARE FOR NEXT SUNDAY

Read **Luke 11:1–13** and study "Glory To God In The Highest."

Sources:
Attridge, Harold et. al. *The Harper Collins Study Bible New Revised Standard Version*. New York: Harper One, 2006. 1693, 1694, 1736.
Bromiley, G. W. *Theological Dictionary of the New Testament*. 7th Edition. Grand Rapids, MI: Eerdmans, 1978.
Carson, D. A. *The Expositor's Bible Commentary with the New International Version*. Grand Rapids, MI: Zondervan Publishing House, 1995.
Fullam, E. L. *Living the Lord's Prayer*. Lincoln, VA: Chosen Books, 1980.
Green, J. B. *The New International Commentary on the New Tesstament: The Gospel of Luke*. Grand Rapids, MI: Eerdmans, 1997.
Hagner, D. A. *Word Biblical Commentary: Matthew 14-28 Vol. 33*. Dallas, TX: Word Books Publisher, 1995.
Hendriksen, W. *New Testament Commentary: Luke*. Carlisle, PA: The Banner of Truth Trust, 1978.
Howard, F. D. *The Gospel of Matthew: A Study Manual*. Grand Rapids, MI: Baker Book House, 1961.
Howard, M. J. *The New International Greek Testament Commentary: The Gospel of Luke*. Grand Rapids, MI: Eerdmans, 1978.
Keener, C. S. *The IVP Bible Background Commentary: New Testament*. Downers Grove, IL: Inter Varsity Press, 1993.
Morris, L. *Tyndale New Testament Commentary: Luke*. Grand Rapids, MI: Eerdmans, 1984.
Nolland, J. *Word Biblical Commentary: Luke 9:21–18:34. Vol. 35B*. Dallas, Texas: Word Books, 1993.
Ryrie, C. C. *The Ryrie Study Bible: New Testament, King James Version*. Chicago, IL: The Moody Bible Institute, 1976.
Tasker, R. V. *Tyndale New Testament Commentaries: Matthew*. Grand Rapids, MI: Wm. Eerdmans Publishing Company, 1961.
Unger, Merrill. *Unger's Bible Dictionary*. Chicago, IL: Moody Press, 1981. 387, 388, 847, 848.
Vine, W. E. *An Expository Dictionary of New Testament Words*. Old Tappan, NJ: Fleming H. Revell, 1966.
Vine, W. E. *An Expository Dictionary of the New Testament Words*. 7th Edition. Old Tappan, NJ: Fleming H. Revell, 1966.
Wilson, N. S., and L. K. Taylor. *Tyndale Handbook of Bible Charts and Maps*. Wheaton, IL: Tyndale House Publisher, 2001.
Zodhiates, Spiros, Baker, Warren. eds *Hebrew Greek Key Word Study Bible King James Version*. 2nd ed. Chattanooga, TN: AMG Publishers, 1991. 1749, 1766, 51.

COMMENTS / NOTES:

LESSON 4 • DECEMBER 22, 2024

GLORY TO GOD IN THE HIGHEST

BIBLE BASIS: LUKE 2:8–20

BIBLE TRUTH: The angels announced the birth of the Savior and a multitude of the heavenly host praised God.

MEMORY VERSE: "And the shepherds returned, glorifying and praising God for all the things that they had heard and seen, as it was told unto them" (Luke 2:20).

LESSON AIM: By the end of this lesson, your students will: EXPLORE the events that led to the angels' spontaneous joy and the shepherds' pilgrimage to see Jesus; feel the unrestrained joy that comes with the good news of the Savior's birth; and PARTICIPATE in worship events of Christmas and Epiphany.

BACKGROUND SCRIPTURE: Matthew 14:22–36; Mark 9:15–24—Read and incorporate the insights gained from the Background Scriptures into your study of the lesson.

LESSON SCRIPTURE

LUKE 2:8–20, KJV

8 And there were in the same country shepherds abiding in the field, keeping watch over their flock by night.

9 And, lo, the angel of the Lord came upon them, and the glory of the Lord shone round about them: and they were sore afraid.

10 And the angel said unto them, Fear not: for, behold, I bring you good tidings of great joy, which shall be to all people.

11 For unto you is born this day in the city of David a Saviour, which is Christ the Lord.

12 And this shall be a sign unto you; Ye shall find the babe wrapped in swaddling clothes, lying in a manger.

13 And suddenly there was with the angel a multitude of the heavenly host praising God, and saying,

14 Glory to God in the highest, and on earth peace, good will toward men.

15 And it came to pass, as the angels were gone away from them into heaven, the shepherds said one to another, Let us now go even unto Bethlehem, and see this thing which is come to pass, which the Lord hath made known unto us.

16 And they came with haste, and found Mary, and Joseph, and the babe lying in a manger.

17 And when they had seen it, they made known abroad the saying which was told them concerning this child.

18 And all they that heard it wondered at those things which were told them by the shepherds.

19 But Mary kept all these things, and pondered them in her heart.

20 And the shepherds returned, glorifying and praising God for all the things that they had heard and seen, as it was told unto them.

LESSON 4 • DECEMBER 22, 2024

BIBLICAL DEFINITIONS

A. Gennesaret (Matthew 14:27)
Gennesaret (Gk.)—A lovely and fertile region near the sea of Galilee.
B. Of little faith (v. 31) *oligopistos* (Gk.)—Puny, small trust, short burst of belief, uncertain of belief.

LIFE NEED FOR TODAY'S LESSON

AIM: Students will discover that people have events in their lives that causes spontaneous celebration.

INTRODUCTION
The Lowly Shepherds

By the time we arrive at the story of the angel of the Lord bringing news of Jesus' birth to the shepherds, several events have already occurred. The angel Gabriel had been sent by God to inform Mary that God was giving her a son named Jesus, who would be "the Son of the Highest" and would rule a kingdom that would be established forever (**Luke 1:26–38**). Pregnant Mary and her fiancé Joseph had traveled at least 70 miles (from Nazareth to Bethlehem) to register under a census by Quirinius, governor of Syria. After the couple couln't find suitable room; Mary was forced to deliver Jesus in a stable, wrap him in swaddling clothes, and lay him in a manager, right near the livestock animals (**Luke 2:1–7**).

BIBLE LEARNING

AIM: Students will know that Jesus' birth was to an unlikely audience in a way that made God's glory visible.

1. THE ANGEL OF THE LORD DELIVERS A MESSAGE (Luke 2:8–14)

The angel of the Lord appears as a heavenly being who is a special messenger or servant of God. An angel becomes visible to accomplish the precise will of the Lord. Beside the stories of Jesus' birth, the angel of the Lord also appears in the Old Testament to Moses at the burning bush (**Exodus 3**). The angel of the Lord came to (or stood before) the shepherds who were tending to their flock at night. The nighttime setting gives an interesting contrast when the glory (Gk. doxa, **DAW-ksa**) of the Lord appears with the angel of the Lord. The glory "shone round about them," suggesting an image of radiating light. This automatically made the shepherds afraid. Just imagine walking at night and a comet suddenly appearing before you. Fear would be a very natural response.

Watching the Sheep (verses 8–14)

8 And there were in the same country shepherds abiding in the field, keeping watch over their flock by night. 9 And, lo, the angel of the Lord came upon them, and the glory of the Lord shone round about them: and they were sore afraid.

As the shepherds watched their flock that night, the angel suddenly appeared to them. The glory of the Lord shone around them. The "glory" *doxa* (Gk. **DOX-ah**) is used here like in the Old Testament. It often symbolizes the presence of God (**Exodus 24:16; 1 Kings 8:11; Isaiah 6:1–6**). It describes the radiating splendor and majesty of God's presence. The glory of God, or God's presence, is seen or felt in different forms. To the Israelites in the wilderness, it was seen as a pillar of cloud and fire (**Exodus 13:21**). To Moses, it was seen as a burning bush (**Exodus 3:1–2**). To the worshipers in the temple, it was felt as the radiance of His glory (**1 Kings 8:10–11**). This same radiance appeared to Peter, James, and John on the Mount of Transfiguration (**Matthew 17:1–2**) This phenomenon was often associated with the appearance of an angel. There is a luminous aspect of glory, as described by the phrase "shone round about them." The reaction of the shepherds was consistent with Zacharias' and Mary's reactions when Gabriel visited them (**1:12, 29**). Moses was terrified when he encountered the burning bush (Exodus 3). The shepherds were all overwhelmed by fear and wonder because of the strange supernatural happening. "They were sore afraid" accurately describes this fact.

10 And the angel said unto them, Fear not: for, behold, I bring you good tidings of great joy, which shall be to all people. 11 For unto you is born this day in the city of David a Saviour, which is Christ the Lord.

Here the reassuring words of the angel, "Fear not" (cf. **1:13, 30**), were echoed. The angel told them not to fear and gave them the reason not to. He was bearing "good tidings (news) of great joy, which shall be to all people." "Bring good tidings," *euaggelizo* (Gk. **ehoo-ang-ghelEED-zo**), is a verb which means to announce, to declare good news. The English verb "evangelize" is a transliteration of the Greek and can mean to preach, especially the Gospel. Hence, evangelism is the act of preaching, and evangelists are those who preach or proclaim the Good News of the Gospel. Euaggelizo referred to any type of happy news in the Greek translation of the Old Testament, but in the New Testament it is used for the Gospel of Salvation, which is through Christ's redemptive sacrifice.

The angel qualified the Good News that he announced to the shepherds. It was "good tidings of great joy (Gk. *megale*, **me GAH-lay**, great; *chara*, **kha-RAH**, joy) ... to all people." The great news was not only for all people, but also it was to actually bring joy to all people. The words "all people" (Gk. pas to laos, **PAS toe la-OSE**) means all groups of people "in the everywhere," as Bishop Charles Harrision Mason, founder of the Church Of God In Christ often prayed. Therefore, this Gospel is for people of all nationalities worldwide and this Gospel is intended by God to bring joy to all people universally. What is the good news? The angel announced that the long-expected Messiah, the hope of Israel, the Savior, was born "this day in the city of David." Notice how the angel described this newborn baby that was born.

First, He is a "Saviour," *soter* (Gk., **so-TARE**), which means a deliverer, a preserver, a liberator, an emancipator. It was a name given by the ancients to deities, princes, kings, and men who had brought deliverance to their country. It is used repeatedly for both God and His Christ, the medium of God's salvation to men.

Secondly, He is Christ. The word "Christ" is a direct transliteration of the Greek, *Christos* (**khris-TOS**), which means anointed (the anointed one). The equivalent in Hebrew is Messiah, which is another epithet of Jesus. In Jewish thought, there were a number of different forms the Messiah might take. For some the Messiah would be the King of the Jews, a political leader who would defeat their enemies, then bring in a golden era of peace and prosperity. In Christian thought, the term Messiah refers to Jesus' role as a spiritual deliverer, a redeemer, a saver of souls to set His people free from sin and death,

LESSON 4 • DECEMBER 22, 2024

During the time of Daniel in 6th century B.C., Messiah was used as an actual title of the future king (**Daniel 9:25–26**). Even later, as the Jewish people struggled against their political enemies, the Messiah came to be thought of as a political, military ruler. Because Jesus' humble birth did not coincide with mostunderstandings of Messiah, the majority of modern Jews still do not accept Jesus as the Messiah and are still waiting for one. However, the angel announced to the shepherds that the cause of the strange event they observed is the birth of the Christ—the long-anticipated Messiah of Israel. The Gospels show how many were eagerly hoping and watching out for the Messiah. Andrew met Jesus and told Simon Peter his brother, "We have found the Messias, which is, being interpreted, the Christ" (**John 1:41**). The Woman at the Well said to Jesus, "I know that Messias cometh, which is called Christ: when he is come, he will tell us all things" (**John 4:25**).

Thirdly, He is the "Lord." The word is a translation of the Greek, *kurios* (**KOO-ree-os**), meaning master. It signifies ownership, one with supreme authority over a person or a group, like a captain or chief. It is a title of honor expressive of servants' respect and reverence to their masters. It was used in reference to princes and Roman emperor. Servants, students, or apprentices in the past called their owners, teachers, or instructors "master" as sign of respect, never their names. "Lord" is often used in the New Testament for God and the Messiah—the Christ. It was the usual way of referring to Yahweh in Greek. Because God's name was considered too holy to pronounce, Jews instead said Adonai ("my Lord"), which is *kurios* in Greek. Here the angel's designation of the newborn baby as the Lord identified Him as the possessor and supreme owner of all creation. Later in the Bible, the Apostle Peter declared that God made Jesus "both Lord and Christ" (**Acts 2:36**). While "Messiah," or Christ (the Anointed One), refers to Jesus' humanity, Kurios, "Lord," refers to His deity as the Supreme Being.

There seems to be a number of reasons and theological implications for the role of the shepherds in the events of that night. The main reason is probably for the purpose of identification. Shepherding in the Jewish tradition was a lowly occupation usually reserved for slaves. Therefore, the announcement was to identify Christ's humility with the shepherds (cf. **Philippians 2:7–8**). The announcement also identified His mission—caring and protecting. In both the Old and New Testaments, shepherds can symbolize those who care for God's people. Christ later identifies Himself in John's Gospel as the "Good Shepherd" (**John 10:2, 11, 12, 14, 16**). David writes, "The Lord is my shepherd" (**Psalm 23:1**). A number of passages in both Testaments use imagery to identify the Lord as the Shepherd of His people (**Isaiah 40:11; Jeremiah 23:1–4; Hebrews 13:20; 1 Peter 2:25; 5:2**).

Shepherds at the time of Jesus were not only poor, but also considered outsiders. Their work, like that of the tax collectors, made them ceremonially unclean. Therefore, the implication is that the Gospel came first to the social outcasts of Jesus' day. This accounts for the recurring emphasis in Luke of Jesus' identification with both the poor and the societal outcasts of His day. He ate with "sinners" (**Luke 7:37–39; 19:7**). He said that He did not have a place to lay His head (**Luke 9:58**; cf., **Matthew 8:20**). He declared that He was commissioned to preach and care for the poor, the sick, and the less privileged in the society (**Luke 4:18–19**). Even at death He was buried in a borrowed grave (**Matthew 27:57–60**).

12 And this shall be a sign unto you; Ye shall find the babe wrapped in swaddling clothes, lying in a manger. 13 And suddenly there was with the angel a multitude of the heavenly host praising God, and saying, 14 Glory to God in the highest, and on earth peace, good will toward men.

After the announcement, the angel did not instruct the shepherds to go and see the newborn, He assumed they would. However, he did inform them how they would recognize Him. They would find Him, rather than being surrounded by grandeur and glory, wrapped in swaddling clothes and lying in a manger. This information was necessary because there were probably other children born in Bethlehem on this same day, but no others would be lying in a manger. As the angel announced the news to the shepherds, he was suddenly joined by "a multitude of the heavenly host praising God." The word "host" (Gk. *stratia*, **stra-tee-AH**) means an army. "Multitude," *plethos* (Gk. **PLAY-thos**), quantifies the number of these angels that appear before the shepherds as a great or large number, too many to count. The host is described as "heavenly," which means they are celestial beings or angels. The heavenly host filled the air with praises to God singing, "Glory to God in the highest, and on earth peace, good will toward men." What does this host of angels mean by the song? What message do they convey through this chorus?

By the phrase "glory to God in the highest," the angels seem to declare the purpose of the birth of the newborn. His birth brings the highest degree of glory to God. Here the angels foresaw the ultimate purpose of Christ on earth, i.e., to glorify God through His death and resurrection. Creation glorifies God, but not so much as redemption. The heavenly hosts not only praise God but they also bless those on earth with peace. The NLT more clearly captures the sense of the Greek here than KJV: "and peace on earth to those with whom God is pleased." Jesus' birth brings a blessing of peace to such people. Isaiah said centuries before that He shall be called "the Prince of Peace" (**Isaiah 9:6**). Thirdly, the birth of Christ reveals God's "good will" for humankind. Right from Creation, God has never willed otherwise. His desires for humanity have always been for our good or wellbeing, and He seeks to convince us of that desire. We can see this through the creation narrative (**Genesis 1:28–31**). The psalmist said, "The LORD God is a sun and shield ... no good thing will he withhold from them that walk uprightly" (**Psalm 84:11**). The Lord through Jeremiah assured Israel of His desire for them, "For I know the thoughts that I think toward you, saith the LORD, thoughts of peace, and not of evil, to give you an expected end" (**Jeremiah 29:11**). God's wish for mankind is to "have all men to be saved" (**1 Timothy 2:4**). Peter wrote, "The Lord is not ... willing that any should perish, but that all should come to repentance" (**2 Peter 3:9**). Here the angels proclaim the wish of God for all for us.

QUESTION 1
How did the angels say the shepherds would find the baby (**Luke 2:12**)?

II. THE SHEPHERDS SPREAD THE MESSAGE (vv. 15–18)
After receiving the news of Jesus' birth from the angel of the Lord and witnessing the multitude of angels praising God, the shepherds did two things. First, they believed the message was from God! Second, they went to see the child. Full of excitement, they said: "Let us now

LESSON 4 • DECEMBER 22, 2024

go even unto Bethlehem, and see this thing which is come to pass, which the Lord hath made known to us" (from **v. 15**). Therefore, rather than delay, the shepherds acted "with haste" (**v. 16**). The shepherds' belief in the angel's message and their prompt journey to Bethlehem are remarkable.

The Strange Event (verses 15–18)

15 And it came to pass, as the angels were gone away from them into heaven, the shepherds said one to another, Let us now go even unto Bethlehem, and see this thing which is come to pass, which the Lord hath made known unto us. 16 And they came with haste, and found Mary, and Joseph, and the babe lying in a manger.

After these spectacular and supernatural happenings, the shepherds decided to go to Bethlehem to see for themselves what the angels had told them. They never questioned or doubted the story, but went rather to see this strange event which the Lord had revealed to them through the angels. The clause "which the Lord hath made known unto us" confirms the fact that they accepted the message of the angels as truth from God. They immediately hurried with excitement to Bethlehem to visit the newborn child. They find not only what the angel has told them concerning the child (**v. 12**), but they also saw Mary and Joseph with the baby in the manger. What happened to their flocks, whether the shepherds left them by themselves under the protection of God or under the care of some other people, the Bible does not tell us. How they found the right manger, the Bible does not say. However, the verb used here, "found" (Gk. *aneurisko*, **anyoo-RIS-ko**), seems to show that they searched before they found the child.

17 And when they had seen it, they made known abroad the saying which was told them concerning this child. 18 And all they that heard it wondered at those things which were told them by the shepherds.

The shepherds were the first to hear the Good News of the birth of the Savior; they were also the first to proclaim it to others. Their message was simple; they declared what the angels told them concerning the child, and what they had seen. Their message left the listeners with wonder and marvel. However, "Mary kept all these things, and pondered them in her heart." "All these things" includes the story the shepherds told—the appearance of the angel and the heavenly host. This story adds to the chain of miraculous events regarding the Christ, which began with the initial visit of Gabriel announcing to Mary that she would be the mother of the Messiah. The word "kept" is the Greek *suntereo* (**soon-tay-REH-oh**), and means to preserve, to conserve something of great importance. Hence, it is translated as "treasured" by New American Standard Bible and New International Version.

QUESTION 2
Where did the angels go after they appeared before the shepherds (**v. 15**)?

3. MARY AND THE SHEPHERDS RESPOND (vv. 19–20)

Mary's response to the shepherds' statements was different from the others'. Whereas they wondered at the shepherds' words, Mary pondered them "in her heart." The language here might suggest that unlike the others, Mary's reaction was internal and private, while the others outwardly responded.

LESSON 4 • DECEMBER 22, 2024

Mary and the Shepherds' Responses (verses 19–20)

19 But Mary kept all these things, and pondered them in her heart. 20 And the shepherds returned, glorifying and praising God for all the things that they had heard and seen, as it was told unto them.

Mary preserved the words of the shepherds in her heart with all the strange things that had been taking place, and she meditated upon them as future events unfolded.

After visiting the newborn, and finding the child as the angels had told them, the shepherds returned, glorifying and praising God. The object of their joyful praise is obvious—the long-expected Messiah is born and they have been witnesses. The birth of a Redeemer brings joy and peace to those who accept Him. Here the shepherds accepted the good tidings. Therefore, they praised and worshiped the Lord, and proclaimed to others the wonders of God's dealing with mankind. Like the shepherds, we are called to declare the birth of the Savior and His purpose to the world. Christ was born to bring peace and redemption. This event occurred over two thousand years ago, but it is still as relevant today as it was then. He came that we might have peace, He suffered that we might be healed, and He died that we might live. That is the message of Christmas.

BIBLE APPLICATION

AIM: Students will know that God sent Jesus into the world as the Redeemer of lost people.

"News is like the new reality show," it has been said. Our culture has become so obsessed with news that you can find it anywhere and at anytime you want. News has almost become entertainment. You can get rapid news updates on your smartphone, Facebook, and Twitter. The unfortunate thing is that we often pay too much attention to stories that don't matter; and the stories that do matter hardly affect us because we've become so numb to hearing them all the time. In our news society, how are we hearing the "good news" of Jesus' birth that the angel of the Lord announced to the shepherds?

STUDENTS' RESPONSES

AIM: Students will respond to the birth of Christ by glorifying and praising God and by telling others.

How can you read the story of Jesus afresh and with joy? Take time during this season to read through the story in different ways, each time concentrating on what Jesus' coming into the world truly means. Try reading it aloud. Another time, try doing a slow reading (concentrating on each word). Read it at home with your family. Read it outside in an open field or area. Read it in a public place, focusing on what the "good news" might mean to the people around you. And finally, remember what it means in your life, and allow yourself to be drawn to worship and praise God.

PRAYER

Glory to our God! There is no other God like Him. The Lord refreshes our spirit. Let us rejoice and be exceedingly glad that we serve a God who cares about all of creation. In Jesus' Name we pray. Amen.

DIG A LITTLE DEEPER
In Awe of Christ Power

Matthew 14:24-26 reveals the profound theological and spiritual significance of Jesus' divine nature and authority over creation.

LESSON 4 • DECEMBER 22, 2024

He not only has authority over creation, this miracle demonstrates His mastery over creation, emphasizing His role as the Creator. It emphasizes that Jesus is not merely a great teacher or prophet but is fully God incarnate, capable of performing extraordinary miracles.

The disciples' initial fear and doubt demonstrate their human limitations in comprehending Jesus' supernatural actions. It serves as a reminder that even those closest to Jesus had moments of uncertainty. This challenges us to consider if we might miss miracles in our own lives due to a lack of belief or asking.

The passage also uses the storm-tossed sea as a metaphor for life's chaos and turmoil. Jesus' walking on water symbolizes His ability to bring order, peace, and stability to life's storms. It prompts reflection on the storms we face and whether we trust God for both supernatural and natural solutions. Where are you with trusting God to do the supernatural? Are you trusting God beyond what you can see? God offers another realm of relationship with us that we must access through faith.

Matthew 14:24-26 highlights the miraculous power of God through Jesus, encourages faith and trust in the face of doubt, and calls us to seek His intervention in the storms of our lives. Are you seeking God's intervention or just riding out the storm?

HOW TO SAY IT

Historicity.   Hi-sto-**RI**-ci-tee.

Caesar.   **CEE**-zer.

Augustus.   au-**GU**-stus.

DAILY HOME BIBLE READINGS

MONDAY
Give Thanks to God's Holy Name
(1 Chronicles 16:35–41)

TUESDAY
Praising and Thanking God Together
(2 Chronicles 5:2–14)

WEDNESDAY
The Heavens Proclaim
God's Handiwork (Psalm 19)

THURSDAY
God's Glory Over All the Earth
(Psalm 108:1–6)

FRIDAY
Our Hope of Sharing God's Glory
(Romans 5:1–5)

SATURDAY
Expecting a Child
(Luke 2:1–7)

SUNDAY
A Savior Born This Day
(Luke 2:8–20)

PREPARE FOR NEXT SUNDAY

Read **Matthew 14:22–36** and study "A Model for Prayer."

Sources:
Alexander, David and Pat Alexander. *Eerdmans Handbook to the Bible.* Grand Rapids, MI: Wm.B. Erdmans Publishing Co., 1992.
Green, Joel B and Scot McKnight. *Dictionary of Jesus and the New Testament.* Downers Grove, IL: InterVarsity Press, 1992.

COMMENTS / NOTES:

LESSON 5 • DECEMBER 29, 2024

A MODEL FOR PRAYER

BIBLE BASIS: LUKE 11:1–13

BIBLE TRUTH: Jesus teaches that nurturing a relationship with God requires persistent prayer.

MEMORY VERSE: "And he said unto them, When ye pray, say, Our Father which art in heaven, Hallowed be thy name. Thy kingdom come. Thy will be done, as in heaven, so in earth" (Luke 11:2).

LESSON AIM: By the end of the lesson, your students will: UNDERSTAND the Lord's Prayer as a model for praying various kinds of prayers; ACCEPT the need for constant prayer; and DEVELOP a more disciplined prayer life as a means of growing a relationship with God.

BACKGROUND SCRIPTURE: Luke 11; Psalm 103:1–13—Read and incorporate the insights gained from the Background Scriptures into your study of the lesson.

LESSON SCRIPTURE

LUKE 11:1–13, KJV

1 And it came to pass, that, as he was praying in a certain place, when he ceased, one of his disciples said unto him, Lord, teach us to pray, as John also taught his disciples.

2 And he said unto them, When ye pray, say, Our Father which art in heaven, Hallowed be thy name. Thy kingdom come. Thy will be done, as in heaven, so in earth.

3 Give us day by day our daily bread.

4 And forgive us our sins; for we also forgive every one that is indebted to us. And lead us not into temptation; but deliver us from evil.

5 And he said unto them, Which of you shall have a friend, and shall go unto him at midnight, and say unto him, Friend, lend me three loaves;

6 For a friend of mine in his journey is come to me, and I have nothing to set before him?

7 And he from within shall answer and say, Trouble me not: the door is now shut, and my children are with me in bed; I cannot rise and give thee.

8 I say unto you, Though he will not rise and give him, because he is his friend, yet because of his importunity he will rise and give him as many as he needeth.

9 And I say unto you, Ask, and it shall be given you; seek, and ye shall find; knock, and it shall be opened unto you.

10 For every one that asketh receiveth; and he that seeketh findeth; and to him that knocketh it shall be opened.

11 If a son shall ask bread of any of you that is a father, will he give him a stone? or if he ask a fish, will he for a fish give him a serpent?

12 Or if he shall ask an egg, will he offer him a scorpion?

13 If ye then, being evil, know how to give good gifts unto your children: how much more shall your heavenly Father give the Holy Spirit to them that ask him?

LESSON 5 • DECEMBER 29, 2024

BIBLICAL DEFINITIONS

A. Hallowed be (Luke 11:2) *hagiazo* (Gk.)—To be sanctified, to be made holy and pure, to be venerated.

B. Heaven (v. 2) *ouranos* (Gk.)—The abode of God, God's dwelling or resting place, also the air or sky.

LIFE NEED FOR TODAY'S LESSON

AIM: Students will affirm that people build intimate, trust-filled relationships by having open communication with one another.

INTRODUCTION

The Importance of Prayer

Prayer is a major theme of Luke's Gospel. Scholars note that Luke records at least 11 instances of Jesus praying and two times where He teaches His disciples how to pray (**Luke 11:1-13, 18:1-14**). The placement of this discourse on the Lord's Prayer is interesting to note because in the last verses of the previous chapter, Luke shares Jesus' sending out the 70 (**Luke 10:1-12**), where He calls on them to "pray for the Lord of the harvest" to increase the harvest for more laborers in the kingdom. We learn from today's lesson how prayer and being still enough to listen, enable us to tap into God's power.

BIBLE LEARNING

AIM: Students will know that Jesus' example for guidance on how to pray in the Gospel of Luke is also found in an example in the Gospel of Matthew.

I. THE STRUCTURE OF PRAYER (Luke 11:1-4)

This particular text is traditionally noted as a passage taught to be recited, rather than a model for prayer, hence the words "when you pray say." However "The Lord's Prayer" is actually "the disciple's prayer." Many of the men who followed Jesus were first followers of John the Baptist, so they were familiar with the forerunner's practices of spiritual retreats in the wilderness (fasting, prayer, repentance). After walking with Jesus they sensed that there was something different about His posture of prayer, and just as John taught his disciples, they too wanted to be taught by their leader.

Jesus' Prayer Life (verses 1-4)

1 And it came to pass, that, as he was praying in a certain place, when he ceased, one of his disciples said unto him, Lord, teach us to pray, as John also taught his disciples.

Jesus' prayer life motivated a disciple to ask Jesus to teach how to pray. The identity of that disciple is not given in the text and the geographical location of the scene is not stated. As it would have appeared discourteous and irreverent for the disciple to interrupt Jesus, he waited for Jesus to finish praying. The disciple added "John also taught his disciples," showing that religious leaders taught their followers how to pray. The scenario echoes the centrality of prayer in Jesus' life and presents the disciple's willingness to learn (Green, 438, 440). This suggests that they wanted to grow in the likeness of their Master (**Luke 6:40**).

2 And he said unto them, when ye pray, say, Our Father which art in heaven, Hallowed be thy name. Thy kingdom comes. Thy will be done, as in heaven, so in earth.

Jesus introduced the prayer with the phrase "Our Father in heaven." The Greek word is *Pater* (**PA-tair**) with the corresponding Aramaic term *abba* (**AH-bah**). The use of

LESSON 5 • DECEMBER 29, 2024

the first person plural "our" suggests that the prayer should be conducted in community with others and it also means that there is a personal relationship between the one praying and God. Christians have a personal God, not an impersonal god.

After the address comes a clause with utmost importance: "hallowed be thy name." Hallowed means "made holy, reverenced." The name is not only a label but also communicates something essential or substantive about the nature of its bearer. The sanctification of the name of God implies two responsibilities. God should sanctify His name, which He never fails to do. It also calls on the one praying to sanctify the name of God by their life (**Isaiah 29:23**). "Thy kingdom come" is a petition for God's reign to be manifested in the world. This has an immediate dimension in everyday life and a future eschatological (death, judgement, final destiny of souls) dimension when God will establish His kingdom at the restoration of all things. In this verse the KJV includes the phrases "which art in heaven" and "Thy will be done, as in heaven, so in earth" but NLT does not. This is because some ancient manuscripts of Luke include these phrases, while others do not. Most scholars think that the manuscripts that add these phrases did so because they are included in Matthew's version (**6:9–10**), so the scribes wanted to harmonize the two passages.

3 Give us this day our daily bread.

The bread could be anything necessary for the sustenance of physical life, or the provision for human need. The Greek word *epiousios* (**ehpee-OO-see-os**), translated as "daily," is difficult to convey because the word has no other known usage. Its only usage in the New Testament is found in **Matthew 6:11** and **Luke 11:3**. Basically it could have two meanings. The traditional one related to time is translated as "daily." In this case it portrays a total dependence on God. The example of the rich fool fits the situation where we are no longer dependent on God but ourselves; he said: "you have enough stored away for years to come. Now take it easy! Eat, drink, and be merry!" (from **Luke 12:19**, NLT). The word also recalls Jesus' warning to let "tomorrow worry about itself" (**Matthew 6:34**, NLT). Others, however, conceived *epiousios* in terms of measure or quantity and therefore assume that it speaks of the appropriate amount for the individual, like in the case of the manna. Both conceptions are important because even in the case of the manna, God wanted to teach the people of Israel to depend on Him. The leftovers from the day before went rotten apart from the reserve for the Sabbath (**Exodus 16:15–24**).

4 And forgive us our sins; for we also forgive every one that is indebted to us. And lead us not into temptation; but deliver us from evil.

The word for forgive here is *aphiemi* (Gk. **ahFEE-eh-mee**), and it is composed of two words: apo (**ah-POE**), meaning from, and *hiemi* (**HEE-eh-mee**), meaning to send. It therefore means to send forth or send away. When used for debts, it means a complete cancellation, and when used for sins, it means the remission of punishment due to sinful conduct. The clause on forgiveness in the context of this prayer does not suggest that God's forgiveness depends on human activity as we may suppose. We should be mindful as Christians that our salvation is not dependent on our good deeds. But, for our prayers to be answered, we need to be cleansed from our sins, because they might be a barrier to God hearing our prayer (**Isaiah 59:1–2**). The context probably suggests therefore that we forgive our offenders so that God will not hold our sins against us and generate a barrier to the answer.

The Greek word for temptation is *peirasmos* (**pey-ras-MOS**). It also means "trial or test." The petition "lead us not into temptation" is not a suggestion that God tempts His people into sin, for James clearly crushes this conception: "God is never tempted to do wrong and he never tempts anyone else either" (from **1:14**, NLT). The source of our temptation is our own desires (**v. 14**). Marshall suggests that "to enter into temptation" does not mean "to be tempted" but rather "to succumb to temptation" (461–462). Keener also, on the basis of other ancient Jewish prayers, suggests a similar reading: "let us not sin when we are tested." This fits with **1 Corinthians 10:13**, which states that when we are tempted, God in His faithfulness will show us a way out (NLT).

QUESTION 1
What was Jesus doing before His disciples asked Him to teach them how to pray (**Luke 11:1**)?

II. PERSISTENT IN PRAYER (vv. 5–8)

What Jesus taught His disciples about prayer was a significant departure from Jewish and other surrounding ancient religious cultures because He reveals God in a personable way. By sharing an example they can relate to, how friends and neighbors treat each other in the time of need, Jesus lets His disciples (and ultimately us) know that God is good, merciful, compassionate, and would not turn us away if we pursue Him for what we need.

Prayer and Friendship (verses 5–8)

5 And he said unto them, Which of you shall have a friend, and shall go unto him at midnight, and say unto him, Friend, lend me three loaves; 6 For a friend of mine in his journey is come to me, and I have nothing to set before him? 7 And he from within shall answer and say, Trouble me not: the door is now shut, and my children are with me in bed; I cannot rise and give thee.

It is suggested that these three verses all constitute one question. The beginning of the question can be rephrased, "Can you imagine..." In other words, Jesus is asking which of them would do what the character portrayed in the example does or wanted to do.

The scenario pictures a single-room peasant home. The father shares the same bed or sleeping mat with the children. For the father to get up and satisfy his friend's request, he must disturb the whole family. The friend who came to ask is short of bread and has a visitor in the middle of the night. It is suggested that three loaves is the appropriate number for an evening meal. The basis for the request is friendship. It is evident from the scenario that none of the hearers will do as the character portrayed. The story suggests that in extreme challenge, when we appeal to friends, they will naturally assist us. It also implies that prayer is an issue of relationship. Indeed, Jesus is our friend (**John 15:15**), and will never let us down when we call on Him. In our need we will find God yet more reliable than any friend, which prepares us for the challenge to trust Him.

8 I say unto you, Though he will not rise and give him, because he is his friend, yet because of his importunity he will rise and give him as many as he needeth.

Friendship should be a sufficient reason for the friend to give a hand of assistance. In case the friend does not value the friendship that much, he will act to avoid the embarrassment to the one seeking or for his "shameless persistence" (NLT). In Nolland's view, God's reliability in comparison to a friend "prepares the challenge to venture with God" (632).

III. PURSUING THROUGH PRAYER (vv. 9–13)

Jesus teaches us how to ask, seek, and knock for the things of God. To ask God for something is to come to Him knowing that He is able to supply. The writer of Hebrews teaches us that we have to come to God with faith believing that He is God and a rewarder of those who diligently seek Him (**Hebrews 11:6**). Jesus teaches that we must come to God knowing He is able to grant or supply our need, and (if we are asking in alignment with His Word) that He will do it for His glory (**John 14:12–14**). If we seek after God, His way of doing and being, we will find Him. Searching for Him is intentional and requires focus.

Seeking God for Help (verses 9–13)

9 And I say unto you, Ask, and it shall be given you; seek, and ye shall find; knock, and it shall be opened unto you. 10 For every one that asketh receiveth; and he that seeketh findeth; and to him that knocketh it shall be opened.

From this example, Jesus begs the disciples to ask, seek, and knock. To ask is to make a request for something that we do not possess, and it may not require an effort from us to receive it when granted. To seek is to look for something that is lost; it might require effort from us to get it. To knock implies that a closed door needs to be opened. It happens when we want to get access to something which is locked. These three may suggest forms or levels of prayers. Green explains that the instruction to ask, seek, and knock is universal. It is an encouragement "to recognize God's fidelity and expansiveness of his goodness to respond" (The Gospel of Luke, 449).

11 If a son shall ask bread of any of you that is a father, will he give him a stone? Or if he asks a fish, will he for a fish give him a serpent? 12 Or if he shall ask an egg, will he offer him a scorpion?

After the example with friendship and the encouragement to ask, seek, and knock, Jesus uses the illustration of a father-son relationship. This means that prayer is above all about relationship. Here Jesus demonstrates a human father's willingness to answer his child's request in spite of his innate wickedness. Human beings are evil by nature; but they demonstrate kindness to their children. It is very hard to conceive of a father who will do such evil to his child by giving him something that would harm him instead of what he asked for.

13 If ye then, being evil, know how to give good gifts unto your children: how much more shall your heavenly Father give the Holy Spirit to them that ask him?

Jesus then draws the conclusion and proves, as Nolland puts it, that "the fatherhood of God is more dependable than the flawed human fatherhood" (632). God will give the Holy Spirit to whomever asks Him. Morris believes this gift of the Spirit refers to the work of the Spirit in Christian life as generally found in **Romans 8** (196). In this case, it may imply an issue of relationship because **Romans 8:9** states "...those who do not have the Spirit of Christ living in them do not belong to him at all" (NLT). Finally, **1 Corinthians 2:12** states that we have received God's Spirit to "know the wonderful things God has freely given us"

LESSON 5 • DECEMBER 29, 2024

(NLT). The suggestion is that we should first seek the Spirit, who will lead us to discover all that God has in store for us.

QUESTION 2
What example does Jesus give to reveal how God the Father responds to our prayers (**vv. 11–13**)?

BIBLE APPLICATION

AIM: Students will express faith that they can turn to God in prayers of petition.

Our Lord encourages us in the prayer of faith as the key to a vibrant relationship with His Father. The Holy Spirit is available to us to guide into truth and reveal the nature and character of God; all we have to do is ask, seek, and knock. What would happen in our communities if we really took God at His word, and through the power of prayer we received the strategy to go into the streets to stop the violence through the power of love?

STUDENTS' RESPONSES

AIM: Students will affirm that God answers prayer.

Jesus says if we "being evil know how to give good gifts to our children how much more will the heavenly Father give the Holy Spirit to those who ask Him!" (**Luke 11:13** paraphrase). As the old saying goes, "much prayer, much power; little prayer, little power; no prayer, no power." We must not be slack in the posture of prayer. As the Lord has taught His disciples, take this lesson and examine your prayer pattern and times of intimacy with the Lord. See where there is room for improvement in your relationship with God.

PRAYER

Precious Lord, we are grateful that You give us the opportunity to pray. You listen to our prayers and respond in Your way, Your time, and in Your mercy. Thank You for Your everlasting love. Hear our prayers O Lord today and the many tomorrows to come. In Jesus' Name we pray. Amen.

DIG A LITTLE DEEPER
The Model for Prayer

The disciples observed Jesus praying frequently and recognized its central and powerful role in His relationship with God the Father. Their request for Jesus to teach them to pray stemmed from their desire to understand and emulate His profound connection with God. In this regard, they acknowledged Jesus as the ultimate teacher.

1. Likewise, we should embrace the Lord's Prayer as a model for our own prayer lives. It offers more than mere recitation; it serves as a path to deepen our connection with God. To follow this model, do the following:
2. Explore its teachings about God and your relationship with Him.
3. Personalize the prayer with your concerns, praises, and gratitude, using it as a template to gain valuable insights.
4. Establish a daily prayer routine to internalize its principles.
5. Commence with adoration of God's holiness, love, and sovereignty.
6. Surrender your desires to God's divine plan and guidance.
7. Pray for your daily needs, emotional challenges, and spiritual growth, including others in your prayers.
8. Acknowledge your sins and extend forgiveness to others.
9. Seek strength to overcome challenges and make righteous choices.
10. Align your actions with its teachings, embodying forgiveness, submission to God's will, and daily guidance-seeking.

LESSON 5 • DECEMBER 29, 2024

11. Conclude with an affirmation of God's sovereignty, declaring His eternal kingdom, power, and glory.
12. In following this model, you will experience a deeper relationship with God.

HOW TO SAY IT

Persistence. Per-**SIS**-tenz.

DAILY HOME BIBLE READINGS

MONDAY
Whenever You Pray
(Matthew 6:1–8)

TUESDAY
You Shall Not Profane My Name
(Leviticus 22:26–33)

WEDNESDAY
Bless God's Holy Name
(Psalm 103:1–13)

THURSDAY
God's Kingdom Has Come Near
(Luke 10:1–11)

FRIDAY
Do Not Worry about Your Life
(Matthew 6:25–34)

SATURDAY
The Lord Will Not Abandon You
(Psalm 37:27–34)

SUNDAY
Lord, Teach Us to Pray
(Luke 11:1–13)

PREPARE FOR NEXT SUNDAY

Read **John 17:6–21** and study "Jesus Prays for His Disciples."

Sources:
Abraham, Kenneth A. *The Matthew Henry Study Bible, King James Version*. Dallas, TX: World Bible Publishers, 1994. 1990.
Attridge, Harold et al. *The Harper Collins Study Bible New Revised Standard Version*. New York: Harper One, 2006. 1770, 1785–1786.
Cabal, Ted et al. *The Apologetics Study Bible, Holman Christian Standard*. Nashville, TN: Holman Bible Publishers, 2007. 1509, 1536.
Fullam, E. L. *Living the Lord's Prayer*. Lincoln, VA: Chosen Books, 1980.
Green, J. B. *The New International Commentary on the New Testament: The Gospel of Luke*. Grand Rapids, MI: Eerdmans, 1997.
Hendriksen, W. *New Testament Commentary: Luke*. Carlisle, PA: The Banner of Truth Trust, 1978.
Keener, C. S. *The IVP Bible Background Commentary: New Testament*. Downers Grove, IL: Inter Varsity Press, 1993.
Marshall, I. H. *The New International Greek Testament Commentary: The Gospel of Luke*. Grand Rapids, MI: Eerdmans, 1978.
Morris, L. *Tyndale New Testament Commentary: Luke*. Grand Rapids, MI: Eerdmans, 1984.
Nolland, J. *Word Biblical Commentary: Luke 9:21–18:34*. Vol. 35B. Dallas, Texas: Word Books, 1993.
Unger, Merrill. *Unger's Bible Dictionary*. Chicago, IL: Moody Press, 1981. 632. Vine, W. E. *An Expository Dictionary of the New Testament Words*. 7th Edition.
Old Tappan, NJ: Fleming H. Revell, 1966.
Zodhiates, Spiros, Baker, Warren. eds. *Hebrew Greek Key Word Study Bible, King James Version*. 2nd ed. Chattanooga, TN: AMG Publishers, 1991.
1681, 1743.

COMMENTS / NOTES:

LESSON 6 • JANUARY 5, 2025

JESUS PRAYS FOR HIS DISCIPLES

BIBLE BASIS: JOHN 17:6–21

BIBLE TRUTH: Jesus prayed that the disciples would be united as they brought new people into their community in an unsafe world protected by God.

MEMORY VERSE: "That they all may be one; as thou, Father, art in me, and I in thee, that they also may be one in us: that the world may believe that thou hast sent me" (John 17:21).

LESSON AIM: By the end of the lesson, your students will: REVIEW Jesus' prayer for the unity of all who believe in Him; EXPERIENCE intimacy with Jesus and God the Father through prayer; and UNITE in prayer for one another and for unity in Jesus Christ.

BACKGROUND SCRIPTURE: John 17; John 15:1–11—Read and incorporate the insights gained from the Background Scriptures into your study of the lesson.

LESSON SCRIPTURE

JOHN 17:6–21, KJV

6 I have manifested thy name unto the men which thou gavest me out of the world: thine they were, and thou gavest them me; and they have kept thy word.

7 Now they have known that all things whatsoever thou hast given me are of thee.

8 For I have given unto them the words which thou gavest me; and they have received them, and have known surely that I came out from thee, and they have believed that thou didst send me.

9 I pray for them: I pray not for the world, but for them which thou hast given me; for they are thine.

10 And all mine are thine, and thine are mine; and I am glorified in them.

11 And now I am no more in the world, but these are in the world, and I come to thee. Holy Father, keep through thine own name those whom thou hast given me, that they may be one, as we are.

12 While I was with them in the world, I kept them in thy name: those that thou gavest me I have kept, and none of them is lost, but the son of perdition; that the scripture might be fulfilled.

13 And now come I to thee; and these things I speak in the world, that they might have my joy fulfilled in themselves.

14 I have given them thy word; and the world hath hated them, because they are not of the world, even as I am not of the world.

15 I pray not that thou shouldest take them out of the world, but that thou shouldest keep them from the evil.

16 They are not of the world, even as I am not of the world.

17 Sanctify them through thy truth: thy word is truth.

18 As thou hast sent me into the world, even so have I also sent them into the world.

19 And for their sakes I sanctify myself, that they also might be sanctified through the truth.

LESSON 6 • JANUARY 5, 2025

20 Neither pray I for these alone, but for them also which shall believe on me through their word;

21 That they all may be one; as thou, Father, art in me, and I in thee, that they also may be one in us: that the world may believe that thou hast sent me.

BIBLICAL DEFINITIONS

A. Pray (John 17:9) *erotao* (Gk.)—To ask for something; to beseech, desire, entreat, or request.

B. Glorified (v. 10) *doxazo* (Gk.)—To honor, praise, to recognize, to bring honor and to make glorious, to give importance; the manifestation of all that Jesus has and is.

LIFE NEED FOR TODAY'S LESSON

AIM: Students will discover how small, intimate groups exist within a larger community.

INTRODUCTION

The Public and Private Ministry of Jesus

John's Gospel provides a more intimate account of both the public and private ministry of Jesus Christ. This apostle's editorial slant is focused on highlighting Jesus' deity (God incarnate) and His humanity (the Word made flesh who dwelt among humanity). John's Gospel was the last one written, and he does not repeat many of the accounts noted in the other synoptic Gospels (i.e., Matthew, Mark, and Luke). He does provide convincing proofs of Jesus' messianic authority as "the Christ," Son of the Living God, Savior and Lord. Throughout John's account, Jesus is portrayed as one who stays in complete oneness with His Father and is singularly focused on accomplishing the Father's will. In the chapters leading up to this time of prayer before the Crucifixion, Jesus is careful to prepare His disciples for what is to come: both sorrow and triumphant joy. He informs the disciples of the coming Holy Spirit who will be their Helper, Comforter, and Advocate (**John 14:16–17, 26, 15:26, 16:7–8**), and through this unbroken fellowship, He will continue to reveal Himself and remain in contact.

BIBLE LEARNING

AIM: Students will know that Jesus gave God glory for the disciples given to Him.

I. PRAYER FOR UNITY (John 17:6–12)

Jesus acts in His role as High Priest by praying on behalf of His disciples. In the preceding verses, He opens His intimate conversation with His Father by calling attention to the fact that He has accomplished the Father's will on earth, having brought glory to His name as the only true God by using His authority (**John 17:1–5**).

Prayer for Disciples (verses 6–12)

6 "I have manifested Your name to the men whom You have given Me out of the world. They were Yours, You gave them to Me, and they have kept Your word. 7 Now they have known that all things which You have given Me are from You. 8 For I have given to them the words which You have given Me; and they have received them, and

LESSON 6 • JANUARY 5, 2025

have known surely that I came forth from You; and they have believed that You sent Me.

Jesus makes a transition here from praying for Himself (**vv. 1-5**) to praying for His disciples. He begins with a rehearsal of His ministry to them. In His three and half years with the disciples, He had given them the words that God had given to Him. He had revealed to them the glory of God—the glory about which John says, "We beheld [Jesus'] glory, the glory as of the only begotten of the Father" (from **1:14**). And He manifested—revealed—to the disciples the name of the Father. This language of "the name of the Father" appears three more times in this chapter (**vv. 11-12, and 26**) in addition to three other times in the Fourth Gospel (**5:43, 10:25, and 12:28**). The word used here for "name" is *onoma* (Gk. **OH-no-ma**), which means more than just a person's name, but functions more like a title to encompass the person's entire identity and character. Such usage of someone's name is still common in most Middle Eastern and African cultures. In John's language, the name of the Father is the Father Himself, and includes all His attributes (Brown 754-756). In the Old Testament, we find "the name of the Lord" occasionally used in place of "the Lord" (**Isaiah 30:27-28, 55:13; Psalm 20:1, 7**). Therefore, in revealing the name of the Father to the disciples, Jesus was really revealing the essential nature of who God is and what God does. He had told Philip earlier that night, "He that hath seen me hath seen the Father" (**John 14:9**). Jesus came to make God known.

In His prayer, Jesus reveals further that the disciples were given to Him by the Father. Thus, the disciples were God's gift to Jesus—and a means through which Jesus would be glorified (**17:10**). Carson observes that,

"Christians often think of Jesus as God's gift to us; we rarely think of ourselves as God's gift to Jesus" (184). The disciples were given to Him by the Father might seem strange since the Gospels tell of Jesus choosing His disciples (**Matthew 4:18-22; Mark 1:16-20, 2:13-14; Luke 5:1-11; John 1:35-51**). However, even for our leaders today, disciples—a title that is closer to students or followers than to members—are given by the Father.

The disciples had received the Father's words, and they had kept them. This is speculative since the disciples evidently did not understand Jesus' mission until much later. Jesus was confident that the powerful Word that He had shared with them in the previous months had taken roots. Carson adds, "They may not yet enjoy massive comprehension and profound faith; but at least Jesus can say that the disciples have come to know 'with certainty that I [Jesus] came from you [the Father], and they believed that you sent me" (184). In receiving and keeping Christ's words, the disciples recognized everything Jesus gave them was from God. These words are spirit and life (**6:63**) and are also the word of eternal life (**6:68**).

9 "I pray for them. I do not pray for the world but for those whom You have given Me, for they are Yours. 10 And all Mine are Yours, and Yours are Mine, and I am glorified in them. 11 Now I am no longer in the world, but these are in the world, and I come to You. Holy Father, keep through Your name those whom You have given Me, that they may be one as We are. 12 While I was with them in the world, I kept them in Your name. Those whom You gave Me I have kept; and none of them is lost except the son of perdition, that the Scripture might be fulfilled.

LESSON 6 • JANUARY 5, 2025

When He offered this prayer, Jesus had come to the very last few hours of His earthly ministry. He had taught His disciples everything He needed to teach them, and now, in the mood of a farewell conversation—one that started in **John 13**—He needed now to pray for them. This prayer takes the form of intercession, *erotao* (**eh-row-TAH-oh**), a Greek word that is translated "to ask, request, or beseech, sometimes on behalf of someone else." Jesus' intercession in this chapter covers not only the 11 disciples who were there with Him, but also many who had believed in Him in the course of His ministry, and many more who would believe in Him in the years to follow (**17:20**). It should encourage the believers of our day that both Christ and the Spirit have continued to intercede for us (**Romans 8:26–27, 34; Hebrews 7:25**). In addition, God expects us to intercede for one another (**Isaiah 59:16**). In interceding for His disciples, Jesus sets a good example of spiritual leadership. Leonard Ravenhill, in *Why Revival Tarries*, said, "A pastor who is not praying is playing." Leading God's people ought to be first achieved in prayer. Leaders must pray for their followers.

Jesus prayed for the protection of His disciples from disunity and from the evil one. He had been present among them as their leader, but He was soon to leave them as lambs in a world filled with wolves (**Luke 10:3**). There was a real danger of the sheep scattering after the shepherd was taken away. Jesus wants them to stay together, and here, He goes beyond the new commandment—love one another (**John 13:34**)—to loving them in a specific way by praying for them. Jesus is showing us here that there are issues in life that teaching and counseling will not resolve without the help of prayer. Even though all disciples belong to Christ and to the Father (**v. 10**) and are covered and protected in this never-changing relationship with God, praying for them was still very necessary. In this belonging to God, they would glorify Christ (Gk. *doxazo*, **dok-SAHD-zo**: "to lift up, bring honor to, and make glorious," **v. 10**). The lives of the disciples would be a testimony to God's goodness to the world, and through this testimony, Jesus would be glorified, drawing many people to Himself (**John 12:32**).

QUESTION 1
Did the disciples know that Jesus came from God (**John 17:8**)?

II. PRAYER FOR PROTECTION (vv. 13–19)

Jesus was there to guard and protect His disciples from the world and the evil one. Now Jesus intercedes on their behalf that they would be protected, recognizing that all but one would be covered. That one was Judas Iscariot, whom He calls the "son of perdition" or destruction, that the Scripture would be fulfilled.

Prayer of Assurance (verses 13–19)

13 But now I come to You, and these things I speak in the world, that they may have My joy fulfilled in themselves. **14** I have given them Your word; and the world has hated them because they are not of the world, just as I am not of the world. **15** I do not pray that You should take them out of the world, but that You should keep them from the evil one. **16** They are not of the world, just as I am not of the world.

LESSON 6 • JANUARY 5, 2025

The theme of joy was critical in the tough circumstances around this chapter. But Jesus prayed in the hearing of the disciples to strengthen their assurance of their relationship with God, and that in being so assured, the joy which Jesus finds in the Father's love may be fully reproduced in the disciples' hearts (Bruce 333). This joy, which is their strength (**Nehemiah 8:10; Hebrews 12:2**), would come through the Word that Jesus had given them and from the memory that He prayed for them on the night He was betrayed. Living in a world that would hate them as it had hated their master, they would need the joy to remain wholehearted in their obedience to His commands (Morris 674). This obedience should not imply that the disciples were robotic followers of Christ. Prior to this prayer, Jesus had called them friends (**15:15**).

This small community of believers would be persecuted in the world, but Jesus does not wish them to be spared from the hostility. He only asks the Father to protect them from the evil one through the power of the Father's name, just as he had taught them to pray, "deliver us from the evil one" (**Matthew 6:13**). In Jewish thought, the name of the Lord is a strong, protective tower (**Proverbs 18:10**). Sometimes, in the face of persecution and martyrdoms, it seems that they were not protected at all. But their protection is guaranteed, they are the apple of the Lord's eye, and whatever persecution they encounter, God was always in control. Since they do not belong to this world, God will not leave them alone.

17 Sanctify them by Your truth. Your word is truth. 18 As You sent Me into the world, I also have sent them into the world. 19 And for their sakes I sanctify Myself, that they also may be sanctified by the truth.

To be sanctified is to be set aside for God's purposes. This sanctification involves their consecration for the task entrusted to them; it involves their further inward purity and endowment with all the spiritual resources for carrying out the task (Bruce 334). This work is done by the Holy Spirit through the Word of truth—in John, Jesus is both the Word and Truth—and is directed toward their mission. Jesus was sent by the Father into the world, and now He sends His disciples into the same world. The disciples need to be consecrated to serve as apostles—the "sent ones." The Greek word here is *apostello* (**ah-po-STEL-lo**), which means "to order to go to an appointed place" or "to send away." The entire Christian community is, and should be sanctified, for it is an apostolic community sent by Christ to be His witnesses in the world.

As Christ was sent by the Father, He also sent the disciples into the world. The mission of Christ informs and shapes the mission of the disciples. The Father has sanctified and sent Christ into the world (**10:36**), and here we see Jesus praying for the sanctification of the disciples whom He then sends into the world. But the Father had sent Christ in the power of the Holy Spirit. His ministry was inaugurated by His own encounter with the Spirit during His baptism. The disciples' going into all the world would wait as well for the coming of the Spirit upon them (**Acts 2**). Jesus commanded them not to depart from Jerusalem—not to go anywhere—until they had been endowed with the Spirit's power. Brown observes that even though the Spirit is not mentioned in **John 17**, this whole prayer can be interpreted in terms of the role of the Spirit (766). Both the sanctification and the sending of the disciples is a work of the Spirit, for without the Spirit, there is no mission.

Jesus also sanctifies Himself for the same purpose of God's mission in the world. This is not sanctification for the remittance of sin or personal holiness, for Christ is the spotless Lamb of God. "His sanctification does not make him any holier, but rather establishes the basis for the disciples' sanctification (Carson, 192). Jesus meant, "For them, I sanctify myself." With the impending Cross on His mind and the disciples hearing Him pray, Jesus sets a basis for the disciples' obedience later by resolving afresh to do the Father's will—which in His case meant death on the Cross. Jesus sets Himself apart to perform the redemptive work on the Cross so that the beneficiaries of that work might set themselves apart for the work of mission (Carson 193). He shows the disciples that the Father's will reigns supreme, and the disciples' best response to God's will is surrender. In this sense, Christ's sanctification resembles the sacrificial lamb being prepared for the offering (Brown 766–767). Christ Himself would later say, "Not my will, but yours be done" (**Luke 22:42**, NIV; see also **Matthew 26:42, John 18:11**).

III. PRAYER FOR FUTURE BELIEVERS (vv. 20–21)

Jesus also prays for those who would believe in Him based on their witness. This prayer can be summed up as a desire for a unity that would mimic the unity that Jesus has with the Father. It is a mutual connection where Jesus is one with the Father, and the Father is one with Jesus. Jesus is "in" the Father, and the Father is "in" Jesus. Jesus prays that they would be as close as He and the Father are. This is a huge, all-encompassing prayer that borders on asking for a miracle.

Jesus Prays for all Believers (verses 20–21)

20 "I do not pray for these alone, but also for those who will believe in Me through their word; 21 that they all may be one, as You, Father, are in Me, and I in You; that they also may be one in Us, that the world may believe that You sent Me.

Jesus continues to pray even for the future disciples who would believe in Him through the ministry of the apostles. He especially prays for their unity, that they may all be one just like He and the Father are one. He had already taught them that by their love toward one another, the world would know that they are His disciples (**John 13:35**). In this love, they would form a nucleus of a new apostolic community that would live its life through the Holy Spirit while preaching the Good News of salvation to others. Their manifest oneness would give public confirmation both of their relationship with Jesus and that of Jesus with the Father (Bruce 335). This expanding unity would generate a multiplying witness throughout the world, and that is how the church grows (Carson 199). While debates about what this unity looks like continue (see Brown 775), it is helpful to realize that such love is possible through God's power and not only human effort.

QUESTION 2

Who is Jesus referring to when He says: "Neither pray I for these alone, but for them also which shall believe on me through their word" (**v. 20**)?

BIBLE APPLICATION

AIM: Students will know that Christians testify of Christ when nonbelievers ask them about their faith.

The text from today's lesson is considered by biblical scholars to be the real Lord's Prayer as we see the passion of the Christ in prayer for all of us. We have to know the thoughtfulness of our Savior in looking through eternity to see not just those who walked with Him

LESSON 6 • JANUARY 5, 2025

during His earthly ministry, but others who would believe far beyond what they could see themselves. Prayer is the most important discipline in the life of a believer to touch and connect with God in Christ as we truly access His power.

STUDENTS' RESPONSES

AIM: Students will affirm through Christ, believers work in unity as God's agents in proclaiming the gospel of salvation in the world.

God has shown us His love through the sending of His Son to die for us. As the church, we must reflect this love by maintaining our relationship with Him and extending this great love out to others. Christ laid the sure foundation for us to be one with the Father by faith, and this oneness is to be manifested in our relationships with other believers. It has been said that the most segregated hour of the week is on Sunday during church. Show our oneness as believers by inviting other believers who are of a different culture or background into your home for a meal and a time of fellowship and prayer.

PRAYER

Jesus, thank You for praying and interceding for us. Your love for us is amazing and a joy in our lives. In Jesus' Name we pray. Amen.

DIG A LITTLE DEEPER
Jesus Prays for His Disciples
John 17:6-21

John 17:6-21 holds profound significance in our faith journey, as it illuminates key facets of our convictions and practices concerning intercessory prayer, spiritual purification, unity, evangelism, communion with God, and the magnification of His glory.

This prayer underlines the paramount role of intercessory prayer. Here, Jesus intercedes on behalf of His disciples before God the Father, exemplifying His continuous role as a mediator between humanity and the divine. His prayer encompasses their well-being, protection, and unity, offering a model for our prayer lives. We, too, are encouraged to intercede for others, invoking God's intervention and blessings.

The prayer further underscores the importance of unity among believers in the body of Christ. Jesus' plea for unity resonates deeply with His desire that the Church stand united in faith, purpose, and the power of the Holy Spirit. In our spiritual journey, we recognize the ongoing necessity of sanctification, a process that consecrates and purifies believers for God's service. It reminds us that titles, positions, or roles do not automatically imply sanctification. Jesus' prayer for His disciples' sanctification underscores the perpetual need for personal holiness and spiritual growth.

Jesus emphasizes a personal, experiential relationship with God is available. His description of eternal life as intimate knowledge of God should encourage us to pursue life-altering encounters with God.

Remember, Jesus commissions His disciples to go forth and bear witness, echoing our own call to partner in the Lord's work, sharing the Gospel's powerful message with all nations.

HOW TO SAY IT

Consecration.	kon-se-**KREY**-shun.
Crucifixion.	kroo-si-**FIK**-shun.
Intercession.	in-ter-**SE**-shun.
Gethsemane.	geth-**SE**-ma-nee.
Sanctification.	sank-ti-fi-**KA**-shun.

LESSON 6 • JANUARY 5, 2025

DAILY HOME BIBLE READINGS

MONDAY
Revealing the Words of the Lord
(Exodus 4:27–31)

TUESDAY
Treasuring God's Word in Your Heart
(Psalm 119:9–16)

WEDNESDAY
Obey the Words of the Lord
(Jeremiah 35:12–17)

THURSDAY
Abide in My Love
(John 15:1–11)

FRIDAY
This is Eternal Life
(John 17:1–5)

SATURDAY
Making Known the Lord's Name
(John 17:22–26)

SUNDAY
Sanctified in the Truth
(John 17:6–21)

PREPARE FOR NEXT SUNDAY

Read **Hebrews 4:14–5:10** and study "Jesus Intercedes for His Disciples."

Sources:
Abraham, Kenneth A. *The Matthew Henry Study Bible, King James Version*. Dallas, TX: World Bible Publishers, 1994. 2155–2158.
Brown, Raymond Edward. *The Gospel According to John Xiii–Xxi: A New Introduction and Commentary*. Garden City, NY: Doubleday, 1966.
Bruce, F. F. *The Gospel of John: Introduction, Exposition and Notes*. Grand Rapids, MI: Wm. B. Eerdmans, 1983.
Carson, D. A. *The Farewell Discourse and Final Prayer of Jesus: An Exposition of John 14–17*. Grand Rapids, MI: Baker Book House, 1980. 173–207.
Meyer, F. B. *Gospel of John: The Life and Light of Man, Love to the Uttermost*. Fort Washington, PA: Christian Literature Crusade, 1988.
Morris, Leon. *The Gospel According to John: The English Text with Introduction, Exposition and Notes*. Grand Rapids, MI: Eerdmans, 1971. 716-738.
Unger, Merrill. *Unger's Bible Dictionary*. Chicago, IL: Moody Press, 1981. 596. Zodhiates, Spiros, Baker, Warren. eds. *Hebrew Greek Key Word Study Bible, King James Version*. 2nd ed. Chattanooga, TN: AMG Publishers, 1991. 1709, 1717.

COMMENTS / NOTES:

LESSON 7 • JANUARY 12, 2025
JESUS INTERCEDES FOR HIS DISCIPLES

BIBLE BASIS: HEBREWS 4:14–5:10

BIBLE TRUTH: God appointed Jesus, the High Priest, as an intercessor on behalf of His people.

MEMORY VERSE: "For we have not an high priest which cannot be touched with the feeling of our infirmities; but was in all points tempted like as we are, yet without sin" (Hebrews 4:15).

LESSON AIM: By the end of the lesson, we will: REVIEW how Jesus fulfills the role of intercessor with God for His people; APPRECIATE that Christians do not stand alone before God with their sins; and pray with thanksgiving for our intercessor with God and TELL others about Him.

BACKGROUND SCRIPTURE: Hebrews 4; Psalm 107:1–15—Read and incorporate the insights gained from the Background Scriptures into your study of the lesson.

LESSON SCRIPTURE

HEBREWS 4:14–5:10, KJV

14 Seeing then that we have a great high priest, that is passed into the heavens, Jesus the Son of God, let us hold fast our profession.

15 For we have not an high priest which cannot be touched with the feeling of our infirmities; but was in all points tempted like as we are, yet without sin.

16 Let us therefore come boldly unto the throne of grace, that we may obtain mercy, and find grace to help in time of need.

5:1 For every high priest taken from among men is ordained for men in things pertaining to God, that he may offer both gifts and sacrifices for sins:

2 Who can have compassion on the igno-rant, and on them that are out of the way; for that he himself also is compassed with infirmity.

3 And by reason hereof he ought, as for the people, so also for himself, to offer for sins.

4 And no man taketh this honour unto himself, but he that is called of God, as was Aaron.

5 So also Christ glorified not himself to be made an high priest; but he that said unto him, Thou art my Son, to day have I begot-ten thee.

6 As he saith also in another place, Thou art a priest for ever after the order of Melchisedec.

7 Who in the days of his flesh, when he had offered up prayers and supplications with strong crying and tears unto him that was able to save him from death, and was heard in that he feared;

8 Though he were a Son, yet learned he obedience by the things which he suffered;

9 And being made perfect, he became the author of eternal salvation unto all them that obey him;

10 Called of God an high priest after the order of Melchisedec.

LESSON 7 • JANUARY 12, 2025

BIBLICAL DEFINITIONS

A. High Priest (Hebrews 4:14) *archiereus* (Gk.)—Head or chief clergy, who offered sacrifices to God and appeared in the presence of God to make intercession for the people.

B. Order (Hebrews 5:6, 10) *taxis* (Gk.)—Arrangement, regularity, sequence.

LIFE NEED FOR TODAY'S LESSON

AIM: Students will often have someone who makes special efforts on their behalf.

INTRODUCTION

Hebrews—A Sound Doctrine to Follow Scholars' opinion vary on the authorship of Hebrews. Many believe Paul wrote it, even though he did not sign it like his other letters. It was counted as an inspired source and included in the Bible. A major theme of the book of Hebrews is showing Jesus as the Christ, the Son of God, in His position in the lives of believers as Savior, Priest, and King through His deity and humanity. It should also be noted that this audience of believers was the second generation of the church, who were enduring persecution for their faith. Hebrews sought to provide sound doctrine for them to follow, to further root them in the faith by teaching Christ's superiority over angels and prophets, including Moses, and His position as the great High Priest.

BIBLE LEARNING

AIM: Students will know that Jesus was the perfect high priest because He was sinless and offered the perfect sacrifice, Himself, so everyone could be forgiven.

I. JESUS THE GREAT HIGH PRIEST (Hebrews 4:14–16)

Jesus in His function as our High Priest puts an end to the need to petition anyone else for the forgiveness of sins. The writer reiterates to his audience that Jesus as the Son of God is the profession of the faith, and that because of Him we are able to approach the throne of God. Through this passage, Christians are invited to stand strong in this belief in the face of those who argue differently.

Jesus is Supreme (verses 14–16)

14 Seeing then that we have a great high priest, that is passed into the heavens, Jesus the Son of God, let us hold fast our profession. 15 For we have not an high priest which cannot be touched with the feeling of our infirmities; but was in all points tempted like as we are, yet without sin. 16 Let us therefore come boldly unto the throne of grace, that we may obtain mercy, and find grace to help in time of need.

The author turns our attention to Jesus as the great High Priest. The adjective "great" (Gk. *megas*, **MEH-gas**) places Him in a different category than any other high priest. He is the High Priest of all high priests. The phrase "passed into the heavens" is similar to what the high priest did on the Day of Atonement. He "passed through" the curtain of the temple and entered the Holy of Holies, where the Ark of the Covenant was placed. The Holy of Holies was where God resided. Jesus' passing into the heavens suggests that He has gone into the very presence of God.

This passage has two admonitions: to hold fast our profession and approach the throne of grace. Both are possible only through

Jesus Christ, our great High Priest. Jesus was "touched with the feeling of our infirmities." This does not mean that He experienced every circumstance that we have experienced. It means He experienced and felt what we have felt in our own particular moments of weaknesses and suffering. He has experienced the same emotions and pain. When we pray, we can also approach God with great hope and expectation because we know we will find forgiveness, mercy, and help to overcome our problems. The mention of the "throne of grace" suggests the area of the Ark of the Covenant which was called "the mercy seat." This was where the high priest sprinkled the blood of the sacrifice to make atonement with God for the people. The author is saying that unlike those other high priests who went into the Holy of Holies trembling, we can come boldly to God because of the work of Jesus our great High Priest.

QUESTION 1
Where can we go to receive mercy and the grace to help in times of need (**Hebrews 4:14–16**)?

II. JESUS AND EARTHLY HIGH PRIESTS (Hebrews 5:1–6)

The writer goes on to draw comparisons to the office of high priest to show how Jesus perfects the custom. Under the Mosaic Law, God set apart the high priest to represent Himself to the people and the people to Him.

The Responsibilities of a High Priest (verses 1–6)

5:1 For every high priest taken from among men is ordained for men in things pertaining to God, that he may offer both gifts and sacrifices for sins:

This section does not discuss all the features of this office, but highlights those that correspond with what the author wants to say about Jesus as High Priest (**vv. 1–4**). A high priest must be one of the people in order to fulfill his role effectively. He is taken from among men to mediate between them and God. These points are essential in understanding the priesthood of Jesus. One of the functions of a high priest is to "offer both gifts and sacrifices" or to make atonement for sin. The high priest must be holy in all that he is and does. The life of the high priest was governed by a particular set of rules regulating his behavior even down to his apparel when offering sacrifices for the people. The high priest was a representative for the people in "things pertaining to God." Jesus is also holy and pure and able to represent the people before God not because of what He wears or adhering to certain ritual regulations but because He is holy in His very nature.

2 Who can have compassion on the ignorant, and on them that are out of the way; for that he himself also is compassed with infirmity.

Another function of the priest is to empathize with the people. Even though this is not a specific function stated for Aaron, it is implied in his responsibility. The word translated "compassion" is *metriopathe* (Gk. **me-tree-oh-PAHthey**). It is used only here in the New Testament and means to act in moderation or to control one's emotion. A high priest is expected to have compassion toward those who are ignorant and "on them that are out of the way" ("going astray," NIV; see also **Leviticus 4; Numbers 15:22–31**). The high priest is to be compassionate toward those who have ignorantly sinned against the Lord. He should neither dismiss sin lightly nor severely condemn the sinner. He ought to act in moderation. Jesus is able to have compassion because He was a man, and although He was without sin, He could identify with human weakness.

3 And by reason hereof he ought, as for the people, so also for himself, to offer for sins.

The high priest in the Old Testament also had to offer sacrifices for himself (**Leviticus 16:11**) because, like the people, he had sinned. His task, therefore, was not to condemn sinners but to stand in solidarity with them. In doing this he could offer a sacrifice for them. By recognizing his own weakness, he could be deeply compassionate toward and patient with those who were not walking in the truth.

4 And no man taketh this honour unto himself, but he that is called of God, as was Aaron.

A high priest must be "called" (Gk. *kaloumenos*, **ka-LOO-men-ose**) by God. One cannot just decide to enter into this high office and mediate between God and people. Since sinful humanity has violated God's righteous law, we cannot select the mediator. Only God can decide whom He wants as mediator. Aaron and his sons were appointed as priests by God Himself (**Exodus 28**). The connection between this office and Christ's role as High Priest is clearly stated in verse 5.

5 So also Christ glorified not himself to be made an high priest; but he that said unto him, Thou art my Son, to day have I begotten thee. 6 As he saith also in another place, Thou art a priest for ever after the order of Melchisedec.

Although Christ is compared to the high priest and they are both called by God, Christ is superior. In verse 4, the phrase "he that is called of God" indicates that the calling to the office of the high priest is an honor that God gives to whomever He chooses. However, a stronger word, *doxazo* (**dok-SAD-zo**), which means "to glorify, praise, or honor," is used to describe Jesus' becoming High Priest. Christ is glorified or exalted to this office. In **verse 5**, God's call is expressed in the words of **Psalm 2:7** (which was also quoted in **Hebrews 1:5**).

Verse 6 is a quotation of **Psalm 110** (which was also quoted in **Hebrews 1:13**). Unlike Aaron, Melchisedec was both king and priest. No king in Israel functioned as both a king and a priest. As priest and king, Melchizedek had no predecessor and no successor. Similarly, Christ is our High Priest forever. His perfect work of atonement is perpetual; thus, He cannot be succeeded. Jesus Christ is the Son of God, our High Priest and King.

QUESTION 2
How does Christ as High Priest compare among the priests of the Old Testament (vv. 5:1–5)?

III. JESUS AND MELCHIZEDEK HIGH PRIEST FOREVER (vv. 7–10)

The writer closes this phase of his argument by introducing the order of Melchizedek and makes the link that Jesus is the High Priest forever. He draws this conclusion because in Old Testament Scripture, Melchizedek has no recorded father, his priesthood predates Aaron's, he is also a king, and he has no recorded end. **Psalm 110:3–5** is a prophetic foreshadow of Christ saying: "The LORD has taken an oath and will not break his vow: You are a priest forever in the order of Melchizedek" (**v. 4**, NLT).

Tears and Prayers (verses 7–10)

7 Who in the days of his flesh, when he had offered up prayers and supplications with strong crying and tears unto him that was able to save him from death, and was heard in that he feared;

Verse 7 emphasizes the humanity of Jesus, which was previously mentioned in **Hebrews 2:9-18**. The phrase "in the days of his flesh" refers to His earthly ministry. The phrase "offered up prayers and supplications" is a reference to Jesus' "High Priestly" prayer in the Garden of Gethsemane (**Matthew 26:36-46; Mark 14:32-42; Luke 22:40-46**). The Gospel accounts clearly describe the fervency and intensity of this prayer. All this shows Jesus can completely empathize with our human condition of weakness.

Jesus prayed for deliverance from death, and He was heard. God's answer was not that He would escape death, but that He would be resurrected. His prayer was heard because He "feared" God (or because of His "reverent submission," NIV). This does not mean that Jesus was afraid of God. Rather, it means that He had the proper attitude of reverence in His duty.

8 Though he were a Son, yet learned he obedience by the things which he suffered;

Through His suffering, Jesus learned obedience. This does not mean that He was at any time disobedient. Rather, He learned how to submit in obedience, laying down His will and rights. The writer engages in wordplay between "learning" (Gk. *mathein*, **MA-thane**) and "suffering" (Gk. *pathein*, **PA-thane**). In doing so, the writer suggests the falsity of the common understanding that obedience always results in peace and disobedience in suffering. Jesus' life and His death on the Cross prove that obedience can lead to suffering.

9 And being made perfect, he became the author of eternal salvation unto all them that obey him;

The phrase "being made perfect" (a single word in Greek; Gk. *teleiothes*, **teh-lay-oh-THASE**) is not a reference to moral perfection but to the satisfactory completion of Christ's role as High Priest. The same word is used in the Greek translation of the Old Testament to mean "consecrated" or "ordained" (**Leviticus 8:33; Numbers 3:3**). Upon completion of this responsibility, Jesus became the "author" or source of eternal salvation for all who obey Him, just as He learned to obey God. The Greek word for "author" (*aitios*, **EYE-tee-os**) could also be translated as "cause." The term "eternal salvation" is to be equated with eternal life, which Christ offers to those who believe in Him. Therefore, the reference to eternal salvation here is a description of Christ's work. His work of procuring salvation as our High Priest is eternally powerful—a perpetual priesthood.

10 Called of God an high priest after the order of Melchisedec.

Verse 10 ends this discussion of Jesus as our High Priest the way it began: with God's calling. It also introduces the new thought "after the order of Melchisedec," which points to His role as both Priest and King. He is a High Priest, but a different kind of high priest. As the pre-incarnate Son of God, He is one with royal authority.

LESSON 7 • JANUARY 12, 2025

BIBLE APPLICATION

AIM: Students will know that Christians approach God with the assurance of acceptance in Jesus Christ.

If you ever have need for a lawyer, it is always good to have one who is able to best represent your interest. Isn't it great to know that in heaven we have the best representation that money cannot buy, but was purchased with the blood of Christ? **Hebrews 7:25** says He lives forever to intercede with God on their behalf. Praise God, Jesus intercedes for us!

STUDENTS' RESPONSES

AIM: Students will model Jesus' reverent submission to God.

Today and throughout the week, reflect on the fact that Jesus ever lives to intercede on your behalf. Live intentionally with the thought that no matter what you experience, there is grace to help in your time of need, and share this grace with others.

PRAYER

Lord, we pray with great joy and thanksgiving for all that You do. We bless You and bow down before You, the High Priest for us all. In Jesus' Name we pray. Amen.

DIG A LITTLE DEEPER
Jesus Intercedes for Us
Hebrews 4:14-5:10

Hebrews 4:14-5:10 contains a profound lesson for believers, emphasizing the significance of Jesus Christ as our High Priest. These passages underscore the unique and vital role of Jesus as our High Priest, highlighting His perfect nature, His role in providing access to God, and the source of eternal salvation through His sacrifice. It calls us as believers to grow spiritually and serve as intercessors in our faith journey. We are encouraged to pursue a deeper, more intimate relationship with Christ and a commitment to spiritual growth and intercession.

Jesus, as our High Priest, sympathizes with our weaknesses and provides a way for believers to approach God with confidence. This underscores the importance of our relationship with God through Jesus, who serves as our mediator. Unlike human high priests who are fallible, Jesus is described as the perfect High Priest, sinless and without any need to offer sacrifices for His own sins. This points to His unique and divine nature, making Him the only suitable mediator between humanity and God.

Through His sacrificial death and resurrection, Jesus became the source of eternal salvation for all who believe in Him. Do not underestimate the redemption and forgiveness of sins that believers can receive through faith in Christ.

Believers are encouraged to mature in their faith and understanding of God's Word, moving beyond the basic teachings and principles of Christianity. Just as high priests were ordained to intercede for the people, we as believers, are called to deepen our relationship with God and intercede for others through prayer and spiritual maturity.

HOW TO SAY IT

Melchisidec. Mel-ki-si-**DEK**.

Infirmity.   In-fir-mi-**TEE**.

LESSON 7 • JANUARY 12, 2025

DAILY HOME BIBLE READINGS

MONDAY
The Grace of God Has Appeared
(Titus 2:11–15)

TUESDAY
An Advocate with God
(1 John 2:1–6)

WEDNESDAY
Our Faithful High Priest
(Hebrews 3:1–6)

THURSDAY
Jesus Prayed in Anguish
(Luke 22:39–46)

FRIDAY
Gratitude for God's Steadfast Love (Psalm 107:1–15)

SATURDAY
Boldness and Confidence through Faith (Ephesians 3:7–13)

SUNDAY
A Great High Priest
(Hebrews 4:14–5:10)

PREPARE FOR NEXT SUNDAY

Read **James 5:13–18** and study "We Pray for One Another."

Sources:
Attridge, Harold, et al. *The Harper Collins Study Bible, New Revised Standard Version*. New York: Harper One, 2006. 23.
Cabal, Ted, et al. *The Apologetics Study Bible, Holman Christian Standard*. Nashville, TN: Holman Bible Publishers, 2007. 1821–1822.
Unger, Merrill. *Unger's Bible Dictionary*. Chicago, IL: Moody Press, 1981. 881886.
Unger, Merrill. *Unger's Bible Handbook: The Essential Guide to Understanding the Bible*. Chicago, IL: Moody Press, 1967. 747, 756–757.
Zodhiates, Spiros, Baker, Warren, eds. *Hebrew Greek Key Word Study Bible, King James Version*. 2nd ed. Chattanooga, TN: AMG Publishers, 1991. 1695, 1761.

COMMENTS / NOTES:

LESSON 8 • JANUARY 19, 2025
WE PRAY FOR ONE ANOTHER

BIBLE BASIS: JAMES 5:13–18

BIBLE TRUTH: The writer of James teaches that the prayer of faith brings healing and offers Elijah's prayer as an example of prayer's effectiveness.

MEMORY VERSE: "Therefore, confess your sins to one another, and pray for one another so that you may be healed. The effective prayer of a righteous man can accomplish much" (James 5:16).

LESSON AIM: By the end of the lesson, we will: EXPLORE James' admonitions for prayer and its power to heal; AFFIRM that prayer is powerful and yields good results; and PRAY for the sick.

BACKGROUND SCRIPTURE: James 5:13-18; Lamentations 3:52–58—Read and incorporate the insights gained from the Background Scriptures into your study of the lesson.

LESSON SCRIPTURE

JAMES 5:13–18, KJV

13 Is any among you afflicted? let him pray. Is any merry? let him sing psalms.

14 Is any sick among you? let him call for the elders of the church; and let them pray over him, anointing him with oil in the name of the Lord:

15 And the prayer of faith shall save the sick, and the Lord shall raise him up; and if he have committed sins, they shall be forgiven him.

16 Confess your faults one to another, and pray one for another, that ye may be healed. The effectual fervent prayer of a righteous man availeth much.

17 Elias was a man subject to like passions as we are, and he prayed earnestly that it might not rain: and it rained not on the earth by the space of three years and six months.

18 And he prayed again, and the heaven gave rain, and the earth brought forth her fruit.

BIBLICAL DEFINITIONS

A. Sick (James 5:14) *astheneo* (Gk.)—To be weak, feeble, without strength, powerless.

B. Fervent (v. 16) *energeo* (Gk.)—To be operative, to be at work, to put forth power.

LIFE NEED FOR TODAY'S LESSON

AIM: Students will know that illness is a part of being human.

INTRODUCTION

James, A Book of Wisdom

James has been called the Proverbs of the New Testament, because it is full of wisdom and practical teaching about the Christian life. This epistle was written prior to 70 A.D., but a more precise date is difficult. James 1:1 identifies the author as "James, a servant of God and of the Lord Jesus Christ" (KJV). If this was James the son of Zebedee, he died in the early 40s A.D. (before 44), if James the brother of Jesus, then he died in the 60s A.D. In **James 1:5**, Christians are admonished to ask

God for wisdom if they lack it, because God gives wisdom freely and generously.

Some of the themes that are discussed in this epistle are spiritual growth, maturing in Christ, enduring temptation, and demonstrating the faith. James was calling the church to practice holy living. He was encouraging the church to allow their faith to be demonstrated in their lifestyles.

Historically, **James 5:13–18** has been used to claim healing. While healing is addressed, the main idea of the passage is prayer. From Genesis to Revelation, countless examples are given of people imploring God in prayer. In the Old Testament, we read about prayers that moved God to act powerfully and miraculously. David offered prayers of confession for sin. Prophets like Moses and Elijah offered prayers on behalf of Israel for deliverance. In the New Testament, Jesus gives a model for prayer, and New Testament letters often ended with a focus on prayer. James uses this portion of the letter to apply prayer to illness. **James 5:13–20** deals with various issues involving prayer. James here deals with prayer of the individual (**v. 13**), the prayer of the elders (**vv. 14–15**), the prayer of friends and companions for one another (**v. 16**), and the prayer of the prophet Elijah (**vv. 17–18**). No matter what circumstances believers find themselves in, prayer is the recommended remedy.

BIBLE LEARNING

AIM: Students will affirm that prayer is talking to God and waiting to hear what God speaks to us.

I. THE EXHORTATION TO PRAY (James 5:13–16)

An initial reading of **James 5:13–18** would suggest that this passage is about healing. A deeper study reveals that the overall theme is prayer. **Verse 13** specifically addresses prayers of the individual Christians who have been experiencing suffering. James asks, "Is any among you afflicted?" The Greek word *kakopatheo* (**kah-koe-pa-THEH-oh**) means "to suffer misfortune" and is not used for illness. During suffering or misfortune prayer is the conduit to our strength. As we navigate the trials of life, we may feel tempted to question the goodness of God and others. Prayer will help Christians to stay positive and keep our eyes on God even in our darkest hour. In contrast, the believer is also admonished to sing psalms when things are going good. No matter what the circumstance, the believer's focus is toward God.

Prescription for Life Circumstances (verses 13–16)

13 Is any among you afflicted? let him pray. Is any merry? let him sing psalms.

James advises believers on how to respond to different life circumstances. The believers experienced times of joy and times of sorrow (**vv. 13–18; 1:2–3**). James urged them to turn constantly to communication with God in whatever circumstances life brought their way, even in going through "affliction" (Gk. *kakopatheo*, **kah-koh-pahth-EH-oh**) as well as when "merry" (Gk. *euthumeo*, **yoo-thoo-MEH-oh**). In regards to affliction, it may not be removed, but it certainly can be transformed. Divine help and blessings are conveyed to the Christian in response either to his or her own prayers or the intercessions of other Christians on the individual's behalf. In all circumstances, it is a Christian's duty and privilege to pray. The Greek word *psallo* (**PSAL-loh**) primarily meant "to play a stringed instrument" and later could also mean "to sing to the harp." It can refer to any sounding of God's praises, alone or in the company of others, vocally with or without musical instrument (cf. **Romans**

LESSON 8 • JANUARY 19, 2025

15:9; 1 Corinthians 14:15; Ephesians 5:19). Through singing, we can express our thanks to God. It is a natural response to the condition of good health, which is recognized as a gift from God.

14 Is any sick among you? let him call for the elders of the church; and let them pray over him, anointing him with oil in the name of the Lord:

In the case of being severely "sick" (Gk. *astheneo*, **ahs-theh-NEH-oh**), when the body may be tormented with pain and the mind considerably disturbed, it is not easy to turn one's concentration to prayer. The word here means to be without strength and feeble and can be applied to any number of sicknesses. In any case, the exhortation is to call the elders of the church to pray over the sick and anoint the afflicted person with oil in the name of the Lord (cf. **Mark 6:13**). The word "oil" (Gk. *elaion*, **EL-eye-on**) specifically means olive oil (from the root *elaia*, **elEYE-ah**, "olive"). Oil is the symbol of the Holy Spirit, the divine presence (**1 John 2:20, 27**). In biblical times, it was used for medicinal purposes (**Luke 10:34**). The prayer for sickness is accompanied by the oil as a symbol of the divine presence in healing the body. The emphasis on "in the name of the Lord" reminds the reader that the Lord is the Healer, not the elders. It is neither the oil nor the elders that brings the healing. The Lord Himself is the Healer. The anointing of oil is done in His name.

15 And the prayer of faith shall save the sick, and the Lord shall raise him up; and if he have committed sins, they shall be forgiven him.

The expression "shall raise him up" means to restore to physical health. Physical healing is a form of redemption. Here James is offering God's prescription for healing and the forgiveness of sins. The Greek word used for "the sick" (*ton kamnonta*, **ton KAHM-non-tah**) is from a verb whose primary meaning is to grow weary in the sense of growing weary by reason of sickness. The verb *egeiro* (**eh-GAYroh**) means to rise up, raise up, or awaken (see **Matthew 1:24** from sleep; **John 11:11–12** from death; **11:29** from sitting). The word is used many times for the resurrection of Christ and of believers. In this case it is used in the sense of being raised up from sickness, in contrast to being weak and without strength, with the implication of not being able to rise.

The clause "and if he have committed sins" does not mean that the sickness is necessarily due to sin. The conditional words "and if" (*kan*, **KAHN**) show that it may or may not be. The Bible does not teach that all sickness is due to sin committed by the person suffering, but it is a possibility (**Mark 2:5–11; 1 Corinthians 11:28–30**).

16 Confess your faults one to another, and pray one for another, that ye may be healed. The effectual fervent prayer of a righteous man availeth much.

Confess is the Greek word *exomologeo* (**ehk-somo-LO-geh-o**), which means to speak out and make public or agree with. The believers are to agree with God and with one another concerning their "faults" (Gk. *paraptoma*, **par-AHPtoh-mah**), which means a "deviation from the right path" (see **Matthew 5:23–24**). There is great power in intercessory prayer. The Greek word *deesis* (**DEH-ay-sis**), translated "prayer," has a more restricted meaning. It denotes a petition, a supplication (**Luke 1:13; Romans 10:1**). Sin is the enemy of personal and community life; it must be confessed before the throne of grace (**Proverbs 28:13; 1 John 1:8–10**; see **Psalm 32:1**). The word "healed"

LESSON 8 • JANUARY 19, 2025

(Gk. *iaomai*, **ee-AH-oh-meye**) has both a physical and spiritual meaning. It can mean "to be cured from a sickness" or "to be free from error or sin." It is possible considering the context that James has both in mind in this verse.

A righteous person is one who fears God and obeys His Word. His prayers differ from those of others by virtue of their earnestness and their helpfulness. The word *energeio* (Gk., **en-air-GEH-oh**) is translated "effectual fervent." It can also be rendered "active or operative" or "working." It describes the prayer that has the power to produce the desired effect. The grammar of the word suggests prayer is inwardly working on the righteous person, bringing them in line with the will of God. The Lord listens to the righteous because they fear God and are aligned with His will and purpose. Before prayer changes the situation, prayer changes the person. The prayer from this person produces the desired effect in much the same way as the prayers of Elijah did.

QUESTIONS 1 & 2
What is the purpose of confession in the life of a believer who is sick (**James 5:16**)?

What does "the effective and fervent prayer of a righteous man availeth much" mean (**v. 16**)?

II. THE EXAMPLE OF PRAYER (vv. 17–18)

Elijah is mentioned as an example of someone who offered up prayers that received answers from God. He is said to be a "man of like passions." Here James lets us know that Elijah was not a superman, and he did not have any special right to have his prayers answered more than we do. Elijah is shown to be a human with the same types of fears and doubts as we have. This is an encouragement to step out in faith and pray. One of the heroes of the Old Testament is shown to be a normal person who prayed to God in faith.

An Earnest Prayer (verses 17–18)

17 Elias was a man subject to like passions as we are, and he prayed earnestly that it might not rain: and it rained not on the earth by the space of three years and six months.

Here the reader's attention is drawn to one outstanding example of the strength of a righteous man's prayer, Elias [Elijah] (see **1 Kings 17–18**). Being "a man subject to like passions (Gk. *homoiopathes*, **ho-moy-oh-PA-theys**) as we are" means Elijah experienced the same things that all human beings experience. This word is the same used by Paul when explaining to the people of Lystra that he and Barnabas were not gods but men of "like passions" (**Acts 14:15**). In using this word, James says that Elijah was not a super human; he was a human being just as we are. Elijah "prayed earnestly" means literally, he "prayed in prayer." With this phrase, James points to the earnestness of Elijah's prayer by translating a certain Hebrew grammatical construction into Greek. The Hebrew infinitive absolute denotes intensity and sincerity. When found in the Old Testament, the English translation usually renders it as "certainly" or "surely" (**Genesis 2:17** "surely die"; **Luke 22:15** "with desire, I have desired"). It is similar to the African American church where someone describes a sermon or song by saying that person "really preached" or "really sang." In other words, James says Elijah "surely prayed" or "really prayed." James wants his readers to know that they too can pray this same type of prayer. All the true followers of the Lord can effectively pray with intensity and sincerity and see their prayers answered.

LESSON 8 • JANUARY 19, 2025

18 And he prayed again, and the heaven gave rain, and the earth brought forth her fruit.

Elijah's prayer for rain to return and water the dry land is an illustration of the sick returning to life after the prayer of faith. A time of being sick is like a period of dryness. But the prayers of people made righteous through the blood of Jesus are efficient to bring new life. The example of Elijah praying for rain is intended to show that nothing is impossible for believers who call on God in prayer. Elijah prayed with boldness and waited on God. We are called to pray with boldness and to wait on God in every situation (**Hebrews 4:16**).

BIBLE APPLICATION

AIM: Students will join with the church in praying for the sick.

We are living in a world with modern conveniences like iPads, smartphones, and GPS. These gadgets are meant to make life easier, but often wind up distracting us from practicing spiritual disciplines like prayer. Our lesson today reminds us to pray regardless of the situation. Praying for our brothers and sisters in Christ will keep us sensitive to one another. Through prayer, we can stay connected to our power source: God. He strengthens us to endure the intrusions that appear in life that we never imagined we would encounter.

STUDENTS' RESPONSES

AIM: Students will pray in all situations, both in joyful times and times of trouble.

This week, spend time praying for the needs of your fellow Bible study members. Please write your prayer request on an index card for distribution to fellow class members.

PRAYER

Lord, the power of prayer is a real and motivating force in our lives. Jesus as You hear and answer our prayers, we are reminded how much You care for us. In Jesus' Name we pray. Amen.

DIG A LITTLE DEEPER
Pray for One Another James 5:13-18

James 5:13-18 invites believers to a deeper understanding of prayer, suffering, and healing, challenging them to embrace these truths. While it begins by recognizing the inevitability of suffering in a believer's life, it emphasizes the importance of prayer as a source of comfort during tough times. James urges us not just to seek physical healing but also to find strength in prayer and praise amidst adversity.

The passage highlights the role of the church community in supporting one another, not just individual prayer for the sick. James advises involving the elders to anoint the sick with oil and pray collectively, underscoring the power of communal prayer. An often-overlooked aspect of this passage is the effectiveness of righteous prayers, emphasizing alignment with God's will and sincerity rather than ritualistic acts like only anointing with oil.

James encourages confession of sins among believers and mutual prayer for healing, highlighting the importance of self-examination, humility, and community support. Using the example of the prophet Elijah, James showcases Elijah's fervent and persistent prayer life as a model for believers. Elijah's dedication to prayer is a vital lesson amidst his miraculous deeds.

Lastly, the passage acknowledges God's sovereignty in all matters. While it encourages

LESSON 8 • JANUARY 19, 2025

prayer for healing, it recognizes that God's plan may extend beyond physical restoration to encompass spiritual growth and deeper trust in Him.

Studying this passage is pivotal to your faith journey to reflect on all aspects, especially these less-emphasized aspects.

HOW TO SAY IT

Anoint.   a-**NOI**-nt.

DAILY HOME BIBLE READINGS

MONDAY
Let Us Seek God's Favor Together
(Zechariah 8:18–23)

TUESDAY
Pray to the Lord for Us
(Jeremiah 42:1–6)

WEDNESDAY
We Pray to God for You
(2 Thessalonians 1:5–12)

THURSDAY
You Heard My Plea
(Lamentations 3:52–58)

FRIDAY
Never Ceasing to Pray for You
(1 Samuel 12:19–25)

SATURDAY
The Prophets' Suffering and Patience
(James 5:1–12)

SUNDAY
The Prayer of Faith
(James 5:13–18)

PREPARE FOR NEXT SUNDAY

Read **Daniel 1:5, 8–17, Matthew 6:16–18** and study "Feasting and Fasting."

Sources:
Davids, Peter H. The Epistle of James, The New International Greek Testament Commentary. Grand Rapids, MI: Eerdmans, 1982.
Vincent, Martin R. Vincent's Word Studies in the New Testament: Matthew, Mark, Luke, Acts, James, 1 Peter, 2 Peter, Jude, King James Version.
Peabody, MA: Hendrickson Publishers, 1985.

COMMENTS / NOTES:

LESSON 9 • JANUARY 26, 2025

FEASTING AND FASTING

BIBLE BASIS: DANIEL 1:5, 8–17, MATTHEW 6:16–18

BIBLE TRUTH: The Scripture teaches that fasting is good stewardship that gives physical and spiritual benefits.

MEMORY VERSE: "But thou, when thou fastest, anoint thine head, and wash thy face; That thou appear not unto men to fast, but unto thy Father which is in secret: and thy Father, which seeth in secret, shall reward thee openly" (Matthew 6:17–18).

LESSON AIM: By the end of this lesson, we will: KNOW and understand what Jesus said about fasting and those who fast; FEEL the value of being connected with God while fasting; and PRACTICE a regular discipline of seeking God by fasting.

BACKGROUND SCRIPTURE: Daniel 1:5, 8–17; Matthew 6:16–18, 9:14–17; 2 Chronicles 7:11–18—Read and incorporate the insights gained from the Background Scriptures into your study of the lesson

LESSON SCRIPTURE

DANIEL 1:5, 8–17, MATTHEW 6:16–18, KJV

5 And the king appointed them a daily provision of the king's meat, and of the wine which he drank: so nourishing them three years, that at the end thereof they might stand before the king.

8 But Daniel purposed in his heart that he would not defile himself with the portion of the king's meat, nor with the wine which he drank: therefore he requested of the prince of the eunuchs that he might not defile himself.

9 Now God had brought Daniel into favour and tender love with the prince of the eunuchs.

10 And the prince of the eunuchs said unto Daniel, I fear my lord the king, who hath appointed your meat and your drink: for why should he see your faces worse liking than the children which are of your sort? then shall ye make me endanger my head to the king.

11 Then said Daniel to Melzar, whom the prince of the eunuchs had set over Daniel, Hananiah, Mishael, and Azariah,

12 Prove thy servants, I beseech thee, ten days; and let them give us pulse to eat, and water to drink.

13 Then let our countenances be looked upon before thee, and the countenance of the children that eat of the portion of the king's meat: and as thou seest, deal with thy servants.

14 So he consented to them in this matter, and proved them ten days.

15 And at the end of ten days their countenances appeared fairer and fatter in flesh than all the children which did eat the portion of the king's meat.

16 Thus Melzar took away the portion of their meat, and the wine that they should drink; and gave them pulse.

17 As for these four children, God gave them knowledge and skill in all learning and wisdom: and Daniel had understanding in all visions and dreams.

LESSON 9 • JANUARY 26, 2025

Matthew 6:16 Moreover when ye fast, be not, as the hypocrites, of a sad countenance: for they disfigure their faces, that they may appear unto men to fast. Verily I say unto you, They have their reward.

17 But thou, when thou fastest, anoint thine head, and wash thy face;

18 That thou appear not unto men to fast, but unto thy Father which is in secret: and thy Father, which seeth in secret, shall reward thee openly.

BIBLICAL DEFINITIONS

A. Defile (Daniel 1:8) *ga'al* (Heb.)— To pollute, stain, desecrate.
B. Countenance (vv. 13, 15) *mar'eh* (Heb.)—Sight, appearance, vision.

LIFE NEED FOR TODAY'S LESSON

AIM: Students will often restrict their diet for both physical and spiritual reasons like Daniel and his friends.

INTRODUCTION
Resisting Conformity

During the conquest of Jerusalem, Nebuchadnezzar, the Babylonian king, took the royal youths to Babylon to be raised in his courts. This included eating at the king's table and receiving a Babylonian education. These royal captives would then be a part of the Babylonian culture and government. Daniel and his three friends Hananiah, Mishael, and Azariah were taken to Babylon to be a part of the court. They were to be trained in all the arts and sciences of Babylon and eat at the king's table. Despite being subjected to a foreign power the four friends resisted conforming to the aspects of Babylonian culture that jeopardized their faithfulness to God. At the same time they rose in prominence and authority and promoted the Hebrew God as the God of all the earth. They were in Babylon but not of Babylon. These four friends serve as an example to Christians who do not belong to this world although we live in it. The first test that Daniel and his friends would encounter had to do with their training. This would determine the trajectory for their lives as pilgrims in a strange land. Would they choose to become fully absorbed into the Babylonian ways, or would they choose to live distinctive lives even while they were in exile far away from home?

BIBLE LEARNING

AIM: Students will know and understand what Jesus said about fasting and those who fast.

I. The Appointment of the King (Daniel 1:5, 8)

Nebuchadnezzar had gathered together some of the best looking, educated, young men of Judah to be a part of his royal court. In order for them to be fully indoctrinated into the Babylonian culture, he started with something basic: food. For three years they were to be fed food and drink from the king's table. We do not know exactly what this food consisted of, but we do know that meat was the main dish. Wine was also served along with the food.

Dietary Restrictions (verses 5, 8)

5 And the king appointed them a daily provision of the king's meat, and of the wine which he drank: so nourishing them three years, that at the end

LESSON 9 • JANUARY 26, 2025

thereof they might stand before the king. 8 But Daniel purposed in his heart that he would not defile himself with the portion of the king's meat, nor with the wine which he drank: therefore he requested of the prince of the eunuchs that he might not defile himself.

The Law of Moses requires that Israelites refrain from eating certain kinds of foods that were not restricted in all other cultures. Only animals with split hooves that chewed cud were allowed, so meat from cattle and sheep was acceptable, but pork was not (**Leviticus 11:3-8**; **Deuteronomy 14:6-8**). Since the foreign rulers did not observe such restrictions, consuming the king's portions was problematic because the meat would not be kosher. Consuming wine was generally acceptable for Israelites, with the exceptions of the priests when they entered the tabernacle or temple (**Leviticus 10:9**) and those making a Nazarite vow for a certain period of time (**Numbers 6:3**). But in the ancient world, both the meat and the wine could have been sacrificed to the king's gods, so if Daniel and his fellow Hebrews wanted to be sure they were not engaging in practices related to worship of other gods, it was necessary to refrain from consuming the king's foods.

QUESTION 1
What did Daniel believe would happen to him if he ate the king's meat (**Daniel 1:8**)?

II. THE ABSTINENCE OF DANIEL AND HIS FRIENDS (vv. 9–17)

Daniel understood the ways of God and had already decided that he would not defile himself with any of the king's meat or drink. This was the first step in resisting the king's attempts to conform him to the ways of Babylon. Next this decision in the heart became an outward action. Since Daniel had gained favor with the head eunuch, Melzar, he requested that he and his friends Hananiah, Mishael, and Azariah be given only water and pulse for ten days. He wanted to prove that their faces would be fairer and fatter than all the other children who ate the king's meat. By doing this, he was protesting the sovereignty of Nebuchadnezzar over their lives while at the same time promoting the king's interests. He knew the king would be interested more in the results and not the means by which the results came.

Favored by God (verses 9–17)

9 Now God had brought Daniel into favour and tender love with the prince of the eunuchs. 10 And the prince of the eunuchs said unto Daniel, I fear my lord the king, who hath appointed your meat and your drink: for why should he see your faces worse liking than the children which are of your sort? then shall ye make me endanger my head to the king. 11 Then said Daniel to Melzar, whom the prince of the eunuchs had set over Daniel, Hananiah, Mishael, and Azariah, 12 Prove thy servants, I beseech thee, ten days; and let them give us pulse to eat, and water to drink. 13 Then let our countenances be looked upon before thee, and the countenance of the children that eat of the portion of the king's meat: and as thou seest, deal with thy servants. 14 So he consented to them in this matter, and proved them ten days. 15 And at the end of ten days their countenances appeared fairer and fatter in flesh than all the children which did eat the portion of the king's meat. 16 Thus Melzar took away the portion of their

meat, and the wine that they should drink; and gave them pulse.

This was a miraculous event in the ancient world. In antiquity, as in two-thirds of the world today, meat was only available to the wealthiest people, so it was a great privilege to be offered the king's portions, even if they were leftovers from a religious sacrifice. To be thin was a sign of poverty or illness, so the fact that the Hebrew youths have gained weight was a sure sign that God is with them.

17 As for these four children, God gave them knowledge and skill in all learning and wisdom: and Daniel had understanding in all visions and dreams.

God not only strengthens Daniel and his friends physically but also gives them the wisdom and discernment necessary to survive in a foreign culture. The fact that God gives them precisely the skills the king requires indicates even more that God provides the faithful with what they need no matter where they are.

QUESTION 2
What was the purpose of Daniel asking the eunuch for ten days to eat pulse (**v. 12**)?

III. THE APPROVAL OF GOD (Matthew 6:16–18)

In this part of the Sermon on the Mount, Jesus explains the proper ways to observe God's commandments. **Matthew 5:17–7:12** is a collection of instructions. Jesus does not abolish the laws established through Moses, but instead he addresses the distinctions between hypocritical and genuine observance (**Matthew 5:17**). Very little is dictated about fasting in Old Testament law, with only the fast of the Day of Atonement, Yom Kippur, explic- itly ordained (**Leviticus 16:29–34; 23:27–32**). In fact, the Old Testament includes instances of fasting in ancient Israel for purposes such as repentance (**Jonah 3:5**), petition (**2 Samuel 12:16**) and mourning (**1 Samuel 31:13**). Fasting served numerous purposes, but in each case the individual or community humbled themselves before God by refraining from food and drink and often by putting on sackcloth instead of their everyday clothing. In **Matthew 6**, Jesus does not eliminate fasting as a religious ritual, but he establishes stipulations concerning the intention of the faster, especially in the case of voluntary fasts, which individuals could practice regularly on Mondays and Thursdays. Such fasts should not be about a public display of piety.

Fasting as addressed in **Matthew 6** and a kosher diet as observed in **Daniel 1** are distinct religious practices associated with eating and drinking. Fasting in antiquity typically involved refraining from all food and drink for a short period of time. Today fasting may involve complete abstention from eating and drinking, or it may involve avoiding certain foods, but in all cases the duration is short and for a specific purpose. In contrast, a kosher diet is to be observed regularly as a daily devotion to God, with occasional abstention from additional foods such as leavened bread during Passover (**Exodus 3:15; Leviticus 23:5–6**). In the Roman period and later, some faithful Christians and Jews further restricted their daily diets as a practice of faith, as with John the Baptist, who ate locusts and honey (**Matthew 3:4**). What is clear from the Bible is that dietary habits are associated with faith practices for Jews and Christians.

LESSON 9 • JANUARY 26, 2025

Sackcloth and Ashes (verses 16–18)

16 Moreover when ye fast, be not, as the hypocrites, of a sad countenance: for they disfigure their faces, that they may appear unto men to fast. Verily I say unto you, They have their reward. 17 But thou, when thou fastest, anoint thine head, and wash thy face;

In addition to refraining from eating and drinking, the Israelites would sometimes wear sackcloth, put ashes on their heads, and refrain from washing as a way of acknowledging their humble situation when they fasted. Whether they were mourning somebody's death, asking for forgiveness for sin, or pleading for help for a personal or community crisis, fasting was a way of acknowledging their situation of loss or need. This is not the type of fasting that Jesus addresses. Instead, He points out that at times people do not fast with these intentions, but with the purpose of calling attention to themselves as pious. The word "hypocrite" in Greek has the basic meaning of one who pretends that the situation is different from what it really is. To make yourself look mournful or needy when you are not serves the purpose of getting other people to look at you and either pity you for your situation or laud you for your piety. Instead, it is better to wash so that you do not stand out.

18 That thou appear not unto men to fast, but unto thy Father which is in secret: and thy Father, which seeth in secret, shall reward thee openly.

The word for secret in Greek is *kruphaios* (**crew-FIGH-os**), and it refers specifically to hidden things, the types of things that only God can see. This is the crux of Jesus' statement about fasting. Fasting can serve a number of important religious purposes, but it should remain between the believer and God because it is not a performance for all to see. Holiday fasts such as Yom Kippur should be observed as always, but voluntary fasts should be practiced not for public display but for true repentance, mourning, or plea for God's help. Everything we do should come from the heart, and God always knows what is in our hearts because God alone knows our secrets.

BIBLE APPLICATION

AIM: Students will feel the value of being connected with God while fasting.

In our society, many people eat all kinds of different diets. Some eat fast food and junk food on an everyday basis. Some are vegetarian or vegan. Others have allergies, while others abstain from carbohydrates. Whatever the diet, food is a constant topic of conversation. Whether it is about the health of food or the taste of food, the topic is always on our minds and in our talk on a daily basis. As Christians, we believe that all of life is under the sovereignty and Lordship of Christ. This can even be reflected in the food that we eat. For the believer, eating is not just a physical act, but also deeply spiritual. We can show this by fasting and abstaining from food altogether or from certain foods. This does not earn any merit or favor with God, but displays the closeness and intimacy that we already have with Him.

STUDENTS' RESPONSES

AIM: Students will realize that Christianity requires one to make certain sacrifices.

Fasting can be a challenging practice for those of us who have grown up in the junk and con-

LESSON 9 • JANUARY 26, 2025

venience food culture. Not only do we eat foods that are not good for us, but we also eat way more than is needed. Commit yourself to fasting at least once during this next week. It can be a partial fast like Daniel and his friends or a fast from all food altogether. We can also choose to fast from television or social media. Make sure to accompany this fast with prayer and take note of anything the Lord may say to you during this time.

PRAYER

Direct us, O Lord, on how to fast. Help us to understand and know why we fast. Remind us that we are fasting in ways that pleasing to You and not for show. In Jesus' Name we pray. Amen.

DIG A LITTLE DEEPER
Feasting and Fasting
Matthew 6:16-18

Within the sacred texts, we encounter profound insights into the practices of feasting and fasting, urging us to reevaluate our spiritual journey. As faithful seekers, we are called to confront the challenges and overlooked issues surrounding these practices and examine their spiritual significance.

The foremost challenge is the peril of legalism. Feasting and fasting can easily degenerate into empty rituals devoid of genuine devotion. Hypocrisy, as emphasized in Matthew 6:16-18, warns us against fasting for the sake of public recognition. This challenge compels us to reflect on our intentions.

Our physical and mental well-being must not be overlooked. Excessive fasting may lead to health concerns, and we are obligated to prioritize the well-being of our bodies while pursuing spiritual growth through fasting. Not everyone can fast in the same way due to health concerns, and we must embrace flexibility to accommodate differences.

While fasting serves as a valuable practice for self-discipline and reflection, it should never overshadow our appreciation for the blessings of sustenance. During times of abundance, the challenge is to avoid excessive feasting, which can lead to gluttony and a fixation on worldly pleasures. We are reminded to practice moderation even in moments of plenty.

Fasting without a genuine desire for spiritual growth turns it a superficial religious routine, focusing solely on outward observance. Guarding against spiritual pride is essential. Frequent or rigorous fasting should not breed feelings of moral superiority and foster judgment and arrogance among believers.

Finally, we must never lose sight of the bigger picture. Fasting and feasting are means to an end, not ends in themselves. They should propel us toward broader spiritual goals, including self-control, compassion, and a deeper relationship with God.

HOW TO SAY IT

Kosher.	**KOH**-shur.
Hananiah.	hah-nah-**NIGH**-ah.
Mishael.	**MEE**-shah-el.
Azariah.	ah-zar-**RIGH**-ah.
Yom Kippur.	yohm kih-**POOR**.
hypocrite.	**HIH**-poh-criht.

LESSON 9 • JANUARY 26, 2025

DAILY HOME BIBLE READINGS

MONDAY
Draw Near to Me, O Lord
(Psalm 69:5–18)

TUESDAY
Help Me, O Lord My God
(Psalm 109:21–27)

WEDNESDAY
Humility Before God
(Luke 18:9–14)

THURSDAY
If My People Humble Themselves
(2 Chronicles 7:11–18)

FRIDAY
Humble Yourselves Before God
(2 Chronicles 34:24–33)

SATURDAY
An Appropriate Time for Fasting
(Matthew 9:9–17)

SUNDAY
To Honor God
(Daniel 1:5, 8–17;
Matthew 6:16–18)

PREPARE FOR NEXT SUNDAY

Read **Luke 10:25–34** and study "Serving Neighbors, Serving God."

Sources:
Boring, M. Eugene. "Matthew." Vol. VIII. New Interpreter's Bible Commentary. 12 vols. Edited by Leander E. Keck, et al. Nashville: Abingdon Press, 1995. 87–506.
Gowan, Donald E. Daniel: Abingdon Old Testament Commentaries. Nashville: Abingdon Press, 2001.
Miller, Steven R. The New American Commentary: Daniel. Nashville, TN: Broadman and Holman, 1994.
Senior, Donald W. Matthew: Abingdon New Testament Commentaries. Nashville: Abingdon Press, 1998.
Smith-Christopher, Daniel L. "The Book of Daniel: Introduction, Commentary, and Reflections." Vol. VII. New Interpreter's Bible Commentary. 12 vols.
Edited by Leander E. Keck, et al. Nashville: Abingdon Press, 1996. 17–152. Towner, W. Sibley. Daniel, Interpretation, a Biblical Commentary for Teaching
and Preaching: New International Commentary on the New Testament. Atlanta, GA: John Knox Press. 1984.

COMMENTS / NOTES:

LESSON 10 • FEBRUARY 2, 2025

SERVING NEIGHBORS, SERVING GOD

BIBLE BASIS: LUKE 10:25–34

BIBLE TRUTH: The parable of the good Samaritan teaches that when the faithful serve their neighbor, they serve God.

MEMORY VERSE: "Which now of these three, thinkest thou, was neighbour unto him that fell among the thieves? And he said, He that shewed mercy on him. Then said Jesus unto him, Go, and do thou likewise" (Luke 10:36–37).

LESSON AIM: By the end of the lesson, your students will: EXAMINE Jesus' teaching about compassion for our neighbors; REFLECT on the connection between serving our neighbors and serving God; and EXPAND our vision and application of service to neighbors and to God.

BACKGROUND SCRIPTURE: Luke 10:25–34; Matthew 22:33–40—Read and incorporate the insights gained from the Background Scriptures into your study of the lesson.

LESSON SCRIPTURE

LUKE 10:25–34, KJV

25 And, behold, a certain lawyer stood up, and tempted him, saying, Master, what shall I do to inherit eternal life?

26 He said unto him, What is written in the law? how readest thou?

27 And he answering said, Thou shalt love the Lord thy God with all thy heart, and with all thy soul, and with all thy strength, and with all thy mind; and thy neighbour as thyself.

28 And he said unto him, Thou hast answered right: this do, and thou shalt live.

29 But he, willing to justify himself, said unto Jesus, And who is my neighbour?

30 And Jesus answering said, A certain man went down from Jerusalem to Jericho, and fell among thieves, which stripped him of his raiment, and wounded him, and departed, leaving him half dead.

31 And by chance there came down a certain priest that way: and when he saw him, he passed by on the other side.

32 And likewise a Levite, when he was at the place, came and looked on him, and passed by on the other side.

33 But a certain Samaritan, as he journeyed, came where he was: and when he saw him, he had compassion on him,

34 And went to him, and bound up his wounds, pouring in oil and wine, and set him on his own beast, and brought him to an inn, and took care of him.

BIBLICAL DEFINITIONS

A. Neighbor (Luke 10:27, 29, 36) *plesion* (Gk.)—One who is near, a fellow person or creature.

B. Love (v. 27) *agapao* (Gk.)—To express goodness and kindness to another as a choice of one's will, not dependent upon common interests or friendship; God's love towards man.

C. Mercy (v. 37) *eleos* (Gk.)—Compassion upon witnessing another's misery, typically caused by the commission of sins (by self and/or others).

LIFE NEED FOR TODAY'S LESSON

AIM: Students will reflect on how people of goodwill take care of their neighbors.

INTRODUCTION

A Test Question

Jesus has just sent out His disciples to preach the kingdom of God and to heal the sick and cast out demons. He gave them instructions for the mission, and they faithfully followed them, and saw the power of God in tangible signs. They were amazed and came back rejoicing when giving Jesus the full report of their ministry. This causes Jesus to rejoice and thank God.

Jesus thanks God that what He has told them has been kept from the wise and the proud of this world. In contrast, it has been given to those who are "babes" in understanding.

This sets the stage for a teacher of the law to ask a question. Many times the teachers of the law, along with the scribes and Pharisees, questioned Jesus in order to test and trap Him. This was done to discredit Jesus' ministry. The questions were usually popular questions of the day or ones in which whatever answer was given would place you in a particular theological camp. Jesus was a master at not only giving the right answer but challenging the scribes and Pharisees to live a more God-pleasing life through the answers He gave.

BIBLE LEARNING

AIM: Students will learn that for Jesus and Luke, a neighbor is anyone in need.

I. THE TEST (Luke 10:25–29)

This conversation is considered a typical one between rabbis and their students. Questions about eternal life were common. Rabbis would often answer a question with a question ("How do you read it?") and affirm responses ("You have answered correctly"). However, the lawyer, coming from a mentality of authority, was not seeking to learn, but to test. As a learned, religious Jew, his response quoting **Deuteronomy 6:5** and **Leviticus 19:18** was the correct verbal response, but the motive behind his follow-up question (to justify himself) revealed the flaw in his heart. There was no intention to love his neighbor, only to maintain his reputation.

An Expert Questions Jesus (verses 25–29)

25 And, behold, a certain lawyer stood up and tempted him, saying, Master, what shall I do to inherit eternal life?

Many readers bypass this initial story of the lawyer (Gk. nomikos, **no-mee-KOCE**; cf. **Mark 12:28–34**, the expert of the law "scribe," Gk. *grammateus*, **gra-ma-te-OOS**)—who tested Jesus as they rush to the more popular story of the parable of the Good Samaritan. This dialogue between Jesus and the lawyer is not only a prelude to the parable, it has its own important place in Jesus' work with His disciples. In the Matthean and Marcan parallels, the scribe asks which is the greatest commandment (**Matthew 22:34–40**) or which is the first (**Mark 12:28–34**). In Mark's account, Jesus answers the question, and the scribe approves of Jesus' answer. Matthew's account is a shorter version and includes only the scribe's question and Jesus' answers. In Luke's writing here, the lawyer asks Jesus, "What shall I do to inherit eternal life?"

LESSON 10 • FEBRUARY 2, 2025

Matthew and Luke say that the lawyer tested (Gk. *ekpeirazo*, **ekpah-RAHD-zo**, to put to the test, try, tempt) Jesus. The lawyer was a recognized religious authority, and he tested Jesus, the unskilled Galilean lay and unofficial teacher, to see if He could give correct answers to tough theological questions. The lawyer tried to trap Jesus, wanting to discredit Him if He gave a wrong answer.

Luke's version does not seek to say which of the Torah commandments is the greatest, but rather inquires about the fundamental princiiple of all the commandments. "What shall I do to inherit eternal life?" One who knew the Mosaic law tested Jesus, not as in Matthew about individual laws, but about what he must do to inherit "eternal life," which is the goal of the entire law (Marshall 442). This question also appears in **Luke 18:18**, where Jesus had a conversation with the rich young ruler. It was a common theme in rabbinical debates of that time (Marshall 442). The word "inherit" (Gk. *kleronomeo*, **klay-ro-noMEH-o**, to receive an allotted share) is key to understanding that many Jews of the time thought that their eternal destiny was based on their Jewish descent plus their good deeds. They believed that their good deeds qualified them to receive a future blessing from God (Marshall 442).

26 He said unto him, What is written in the law? how readest thou? 27 And he answering said, Thou shalt love the Lord thy God with all thy heart, and with all thy soul, and with all thy strength, and with all thy mind; and thy neighbour as thyself.

Jesus answers the lawyer's question with two questions, taking him to the Old Testament whose authority the lawyer would not question, being an expert in the same. Marshall observes that some scholars believe that Jesus' question is actually, "How do you recite?" Thus the lawyer recalls the Shema from **Deuteronomy 6**, which he probably recited daily. However, Jesus is asking for more than just a recitation. He wants the lawyer to state his own interpretation of the Scriptures, thereby shifting the dialogue from Jesus' teaching to the lawyer's interpretation of the law. Correctly, the lawyer recited two commandments: love God (**Deuteronomy 6:5**) and love your neighbor (**Leviticus 19:18**). Together these two commandments formed the heart of the Jewish religion (Marshall 443–444), but they also formed the core of Jesus' own teaching. Thus, Jesus and the lawyer end up at the same place in their conversation.

28 And he said unto him, Thou hast answered right: this do, and thou shalt live. 29 But he, willing to justify himself, said unto Jesus, And who is my neighbour?

Jesus observes that the lawyer is right in his interpretation, and tells him, "Do this, and you will live." However, having answered the question correctly, the lawyer asks for clarification, possibly to test Jesus further. Since loving your neighbor is a matter of life and death, the correct definition of a neighbor is of extreme importance. So, the lawyer asks, "Who is my neighbor?" In other words, he was saying, "Whom do I love?" Scholars agree that the general Jewish sense of the neighbor at the time was limited to members of the same people, religious communities, fellow Jews, or fellow members of the covenant (Marshall 444, 446). Marshall adds that there was a tendency among the Pharisees to exclude Samaritans, foreigners, and other ordinary people from the definition (444). Plummer observes that a Jew "except[ed] all Gentiles when he spoke of his neighbor" (285). Since the lawyer might have been a Pharisee, he could easily interpret the commandments in this exclusive manner. He agreed on loving neighbor, but he sought to define neighbor to include only Jews. He wanted to define neighbor—which then defines for him who is not a neighbor.

This question is of extreme relevance in our world where segregation tears the body of Christ apart just as much as it does any other community. Unity in diversity is a thorny subject even among Christians. Divisions take many forms and are prevalent in our communities according to religion, race, ethnicity, gender, age, race, disability or sexual orientation. Black, White, Hispanic, Asian, gay, straight, Orthodox, Pentecostal, Roman Catholic, Lutheran, Evangelicals, Northerners, Southerners, Democrats, Republicans, Israelites, Palestinians, male, female, rich, poor, educated, and uneducated, migrants, us, and them are categories we classify our neighbors, usually to choose which neighbor to recognize or not recognize. Unfortunately, these discriminating definitions of neighbors affect the church's understanding of its mission in the world. God's mission is focused on unity to invite all people into His kingdom without regard to our man-made qualifiers.

QUESTION 1

What does the lawyer say is the way to inherit eternal life? How consuming is the pursuit (**Luke 10:27**)?

II. THE PARABLE (vv. 30–34)

As an illustration of neighborly love, Jesus tells this parable. During Jesus' time, Jewish religion and culture dictated that "good" Jews avoid impure things and people. Samaritans, as "mixed breeds," would fall into this category. Priests and Levites (along with Pharisees) were considered "holy" ones, striving to maintain the appearance of righteousness.

The Neighborly Act of Compassion (verses 30–34)

30 And Jesus answering said, A certain man went down from Jerusalem to Jericho, and fell among thieves, which stripped him of his raiment, and wounded him, and departed, leaving him half dead. 31 And by chance there came down a certain priest that way: and when he saw him, he passed by on the other side. 32 And likewise a Levite, when he was at the place, came and looked on him, and passed by on the other side.

The conversation takes a twist as Jesus brings in a parable to drive the lesson home. In the parable, a man (supposedly a Jew) went down from Jerusalem to Jericho—a journey along a road that descends over 3,000 feet through treacherous desert and dangerous rocky country that could easily hide bandits. On his way, the man met robbers who vandalized him, stripped him, and left him half-dead. While he lay half-conscious on the wayside, a priest and a Levite passed by, and upon seeing him, they went on the other side of the road. Both the priest and the Levite were well-known religious figures. The priests were descendants of Aaron and were responsible for everything to do with temple worship. Levites were a tribe of descendants of Levi but not of Aaron (who was also a descendant of Levi), and they assisted the priests in the temple. The Levite in this story seems overly inconsiderate as he "came and looked" at the wounded man and proceeded without offering help. Jesus' audience, however, might have expected that at the sight of a wounded fellow Jew, both the priest and the Levite would stop by to help him. There could be several reasons for their lack of action, among them: (1) their religious responsibilities may have prevented them from helping the wounded man since he might have appeared dead, as the law prohibited them from touching a corpse, (2) they might have been afraid of being attacked by the same robbers, and (3) they might have simply wanted nothing to do with the wounded person. It is possible that they were not indifferent to the wounded man, but their compassion might have been overcome by their commitment to religious purity.

33 But a certain Samaritan, as he journeyed, came where he was: and when he saw him, he had compassion on him, 34 And went to him, and bound up his wounds, pouring in oil and wine, and set him on his own beast, and brought him to an inn, and took care of him.

The plot of the story invites the audience to expect a Jewish layman to be the third traveler who responds to the wounded man, but Jesus brings a very unlikely person from a community hated by the Jews into the story—a certain Samaritan. The relationship between Jews and Samaritans was one of constant hostility. The Jews considered the Samaritans to be second-class citizens, the half-breed descendants of Jews who had intermarried with foreigners (see **2 Kings 17:24–40**). We have a Samaritan traveling in Jewish territory. His attending to the wounded Jew jeopardized his life, because he could have been easily blamed for the robbery. In addition, the Samaritans were bound by the same religious laws that bound the Jews, and therefore, the Samaritan risked defilement to take care of the possibly dead man—bandaging his wounds, pouring on oil and wine. Being a Samaritan, he could not expect any such kindness from the Jews. But unlike the priest and Levite, he fulfilled the law, showed compassion, and helped the wounded man.

He was moved by compassion—the same powerful emotion that moved Jesus to ministry, feeding the hungry and healing the sick, when He saw the multitudes weary and scattered like sheep without a shepherd (**Matthew 9:36–38, 14:14; Mark 8:2**). The word "compassion" here comes from the Greek word splangchizomai (**splonk-NEED-zo-meye**) which means "to be moved in one's gut, to be moved with compassion, have compassion" (the guts—inward parts, entrails—were thought to be the seat of love and pity). Jesus uses the story to contrast the lack of compassion shown by two members of the Jewish priesthood toward an unknown and unfortunate sufferer with the obedience to the law shown in practical compassion by the most unlikely of men, a Samaritan. Any Jew would be deeply humiliated for such an enemy of the Jews to show compassion to an injured Jew and pay expenses for his recuperation, while two Jewish religious officials did not. The mercy of the Samaritan made him give generously of his own supplies for the life of the wounded stranger: his oil and wine to cleanse and soothe the wounds, his bandage to bind them, and his own animal to carry the man. He also used his own money to pay for his care at the inn, promising to pay for any further expenses the man's care would require. The personhood of priest and the Levite would be diminished for not giving of themselves to help the needy. Love humanizes both the giver and the receiver—and that is what it takes to be a neighbor. Jesus finishes the conversation by telling the lawyer, "Go and do likewise." In other words, Jesus is saying, "Go and be a good neighbor; this is how you inherit eternal life."

QUESTION 2
What is implied to be one way for the lawyer to show love toward his neighbor (**v. 34**)?

LESSON 10 • FEBRUARY 2, 2025

BIBLE APPLICATION

AIM: Students will understand that neighborliness is an expression of one's love of God and love of others.

There are many examples of the lack of mercy and love in our society like selfish, money-hungry executives who choose to lay off hardworking employees while accepting million-dollar bonuses. Too many managers today are taking advantage of funds designated to help those in need. However, the opposite is true as well. There are tales of "heroes," people who rise up during tragedies to rescue, tend to, and provide for complete strangers. It is often said that this is the reflection of the good in humanity and a reflection of God's love and mercy. Without Him, there would be no "good" in humanity.

STUDENTS' RESPONSES

AIM: Students will affirm that those who show mercy without expecting rewards or repayment are indeed heirs of the kingdom of God.

We are often faced with unexpected opportunities to serve our neighbors. There are people with needs all around us, and we have specific resources to help. Whom is God impressing upon you to serve? What opportunities have you been presented with that you have chosen to ignore because it will cost you time, money, energy, or comfort? Ask God to reveal these to you. Pray that He would give you greater awareness of those around you and a boldness to serve in spite of difficulty.

PRAYER

Lord, serving others is what we are called to do. Give us the resources and the compassion to care for others. Guide us put our faith into action. In Jesus' Name we pray. Amen.

DIG A LITTLE DEEPER

Within the parable of the Good Samaritan, we unearth invaluable truths often underestimated but profoundly relevant to our journey of serving others and serving God.

At its core, this parable offers insight into the Great Commandment. When an expert in the law questions Jesus about inheriting eternal life, Jesus underscores the foundational importance of loving God with our entire being and loving our neighbors as ourselves. This establishes an unbreakable connection between serving others and serving God, encapsulating the very essence of our faith.

This narrative reshapes our understanding of neighborly love. The expert's query about defining a neighbor prompts Jesus to redefine the concept. It becomes evident that serving others extends beyond proximity and calls us to extend compassion and give tangible assistance when needed.

While the priest and Levite, who were expected to help, pass by the injured man, the Samaritan, often marginalized and despised, demonstrates true mercy and service. Authentic service is not always convenient and may transcend biases.

Furthermore, the parable underscores the cost of love. The Samaritan not only tends to the man's wounds but also bears the expenses for his care. Serving others may demand sacrifices and generosity.

Ultimately, Jesus' words, "go and do likewise," convey that serving others holds eternal significance. It aligns perfectly with God's desire for His followers to manifest His love and compassion in the world, implying that acts of service possess enduring spiritual value. Let us heed the challenge and live out our faith through selfless acts of love and service to others.

LESSON 10 • FEBRUARY 2, 2025

HOW TO SAY IT

Compassion.	com-**PA**-shun.
Empathy.	em-pa-**THEE**.
Samaritan.	sa-**MARE**-ih-tin.
Levite.	**LEE**-vite.
Ubuntu.	u-boon-**TOO**.

DAILY HOME BIBLE READINGS

MONDAY
Faith Must Express Itself in Works
(James 2:14–26)

TUESDAY
Jesus and the Religious Leaders
(Matthew 23)

WEDNESDAY
Jesus and the Religious Leaders
(Matthew 23)

THURSDAY
Love God with All Your Heart
(Deuteronomy 6:1–8)

FRIDAY
The Widow Who Gave Her All
(Luke 21:1–4)

SATURDAY
The Canaanite Woman's Faith
(Matthew 15:21–28)

SUNDAY
The Suffering Messiah
(Isaiah 53:1–12)

PREPARE FOR NEXT SUNDAY

Read **Matthew 25:31–46** and study "Serving the Least."

Sources:
Cosby, Michael R. Portraits of Jesus: An Inductive Approach to the Gospels. 1st ed. Louisville, KY: Westminster John Knox Press, 1999. 86–87.
Dunn, James D. G., and J. W. Rogerson. Eerdmans Commentary on the Bible. Grand Rapids, MI: W.B. Eerdmans, 2003.
Hebrew-Greek Key Word Study Bible, King James Version. Chattanooga, TN: AMG Publishers, Inc., 1991.
Josephus. The Antiquities of the Jews. 18.2.2.
Keener, Craig S. The IVP Bible Background Commentary: New Testament. Downers Grove, IL: Intervarsity Press, 1993. 217–218.
Marshall, I. Howard. The Gospel of Luke: A Commentary on the Greek Text. Grand Rapids, MI: Eerdmans, 1978. 440–450.
Plummer, Alfred. A Critical and Exegetical Commentary on the Gospel According to St. Luke. 5th ed. Edinburgh: T. & T. Clark, 1975. 283–288.
Radmacher, Earl D., ed. Nelson Study Bible, New King James Version. Nashville, TN: Thomas Nelson Publishers, 1997. 1618–1619, 1714–1715.
Ryrie, Charles C. Ryrie Study Bible, New International Version. Chicago, IL: Moody Press, 1986. 1423.
Thompson, Richard P., and Thomas E. Phillips. Literary Studies in Luke-Acts: Essays in Honor of Joseph B. Tyson. Macon, GA: Mercer University Press, 1998.
Unger, Merrill F. The New Unger's Bible Dictionary. Chicago, IL: Moody Press, 1988. 762–765, 1116–1119.
Walvoord, John F., and Roy B. Zuck, eds. The Bible Knowledge Commentary: New Testament. Wheaton, IL: Victor Books, SP Publications, Inc., 1983. 233–234.

COMMENTS / NOTES:

_____
_____
_____
_____
_____
_____
_____
_____
_____
_____
_____
_____
_____
_____
_____
_____
_____
_____
_____
_____

LESSON 11 • FEBRUARY 9, 2025

SERVING THE LEAST

BIBLE BASIS: MATTHEW 25:31–46

BIBLE TRUTH: Believers should serve others as if they were the Lord, and God will judge the believers accordingly.

MEMORY VERSE: "And the King shall answer and say unto them, Verily I say unto you, Inasmuch as ye have done it unto one of the least of these my brethren, ye have done it unto me" (Matthew 25:40).

LESSON AIM: By the end of the lesson, your students will: UNDERSTAND Jesus' comments on our obligation to meet the needs of the less fortunate; EXPERIENCE how God's love for all inspires us to meet others' needs; and PARTICIPATE in serving the needs of others.

BACKGROUND SCRIPTURE: Matthew 25:31–46; Psalm 10:12–18—Read and incorporate the insights gained from the Background Scriptures into your study of the lesson.

LESSON SCRIPTURE

MATTHEW 25:31–46, KJV

31 When the Son of man shall come in his glory, and all the holy angels with him, then shall he sit upon the throne of his glory:

32 And before him shall be gathered all nations: and he shall separate them one from another, as a shepherd divideth his sheep from the goats:

33 And he shall set the sheep on his right hand, but the goats on the left.

34 Then shall the King say unto them on his right hand, Come, ye blessed of my Father, inherit the kingdom prepared for you from the foundation of the world:

35 For I was an hungred, and ye gave me meat: I was thirsty, and ye gave me drink: I was a stranger, and ye took me in:

36 Naked, and ye clothed me: I was sick, and ye visited me: I was in prison, and ye came unto me.

37 Then shall the righteous answer him, saying, Lord, when saw we thee an hungred, and fed thee? or thirsty, and gave thee drink?

38 When saw we thee a stranger, and took thee in? or naked, and clothed thee?

39 Or when saw we thee sick, or in prison, and came unto thee?

40 And the King shall answer and say unto them, Verily I say unto you, Inasmuch as ye have done it unto one of the least of these my brethren, ye have done it unto me.

41 Then shall he say also unto them on the left hand, Depart from me, ye cursed, into everlasting fire, prepared for the devil and his angels:

42 For I was an hungred, and ye gave me no meat: I was thirsty, and ye gave me no drink:

43 I was a stranger, and ye took me not in: naked, and ye clothed me not: sick, and in prison, and ye visited me not.

44 Then shall they also answer him, saying, Lord, when saw we thee an hungred, or athirst, or a stranger, or naked, or sick, or in prison, and did not minister unto thee?

LESSON 11 • FEBRUARY 9, 2025

45 Then shall he answer them, saying, Verily I say unto you, Inasmuch as ye did it not to one of the least of these, ye did it not to me.

46 And these shall go away into everlasting punishment: but the righteous into life eternal.

BIBLICAL DEFINITIONS

A. Separate (Matthew 25:32) *aphorizo* (Gk.)—To set a boundary, divide.

B. Cursed (v. 41) *kataraomai* (Gk.)— Given over to destruction; to be judged and punished, rejected by God.

LIFE NEED FOR TODAY'S LESSON

AIM: Students will understand how opportunities for serving others are all around us, even though believers do not recognize or respond to them.

INTRODUCTION

The End Times

After discussions with Jewish leaders, the disciples asked Christ two follow-up questions in **24:3**: "…When will this (the destruction of the temple) happen and what will be the sign of your coming and of the end of the age?" Matthew **24:4–25:46**, known as the Olivet Discourse, is His response. Christ describes end times for both Jews and Gentiles. He begins by prophesying the destruction of the temple in Jerusalem, lays out some of the signs of the end, informs them of His return, and shares parables to encourage preparation. He concludes with this passage on the actions and judgement of the righteous and unrighteous.

There is a debate based on the story's implication that our actions earn us eternal life or eternal punishment. It is written, "For God so loved the world…, that whosoever believeth in him should… have eternal life" (**John 3:16**). Paul says, "For it is by grace you have been saved, through faith—and this not from yourselves, it is the gift of God—not by works, so that no one can boast" (**Ephesians 2:8–9**). Faith in Christ leads to eternal life. Showing mercy and serving the poor is a by-product of a life of faith. This passage is an illustration of James' writing "What good is it, dear brothers and sisters, if you say you have faith but don't show it by your actions?... So you see, faith by itself isn't enough. Unless it produces good deeds, it is dead and useless" (**James 2:14, 17**, NLT). Those who love Christ demonstrate it by their actions —by loving others.

BIBLE LEARNING

AIM: Students will learn that the righteous (sheep) will be separated from the unrighteous (goats).

I. THE SEPARATION (Matthew 25:31–33)

Jesus is describing His future return as the Son of Man "in his glory," accompanied by angels. This verse shows how He is both man and God. During that time, He will come as King, judging all people from all nations, based upon their righteousness.

Jesus' Second Coming (verses 31–33)

31 When the Son of man shall come in his glory, and all the holy angels with

LESSON 11 • FEBRUARY 9, 2025

him, then shall he sit upon the throne of his glory: 32 and before him shall be gathered all nations; and he shall separate them one from another, as a shepherd divideth his sheep from the goats: 33 and he shall set the sheep on his right hand, but the goats on the left.

This passage of Scripture is not so much a par-able as it is prophecy. It does have some parabolic traits for it details the shepherd, sheep, and goats. The point here is to describe the events of Jesus' second coming. When Christ returns, He will come back in His full glory, the same glory that clothed Him before He descended from heaven. His angels will accompany Him and will help gather all the people together at the same time. The Jews and Gentiles will not assemble in two different groups. Every nation will receive the same judgment before God.

Once more, Jesus teaches in a context with which the Jews were familiar. Sheep are usually milder and gentler while goats are more unruly and boisterous. Both animals grazed together during the daytime but were separated at night. In this passage, the sheep go one way and the goats go another. The right side symbolizes blessing, honor, and favor; the left side symbolizes worthlessness and condemnation.

II. THE BLESSED (vv. 34–40)

Christ speaks well of those who are righteous, saying they are blessed heirs with rights to the kingdom. This blessing is connected to the outward expression of their faith: caring for strangers in need. His disciples would have understood this to be a basic expectation: Jews were commanded to care for those less fortunate—the hungry, thirsty, naked, imprisoned.

Jesus is the King (verses 34–40)

34 Then shall the King say unto them on his right hand, Come, ye blessed of my Father, inherit the kingdom prepared for you from the foundation of the world:

Here, Jesus refers to Himself as "King" for the first and only time in Scripture. He called Himself by other titles, and in so doing used the first person, e.g., "I am the good shepherd." In this verse, He uses the third person. Although this is in the third person, we know that Jesus is referring to Himself since the King in this passage refers to God as "my Father."

Once the sheep completely separated, Jesus will address them, inviting them into God's kingdom. Matthew uses the Greek word *kleronomeo* (**klay-roe-no-MEH-o**), meaning "to inherit or possess," signaling to the sheep to take possession of the kingdom. Jesus calls them blessed, not because of what they received (grace), but for what they did with what they received. He further says that this place has been prepared specifically for them since the beginning of the world.

35 for I was an hungered, and ye gave me meat: I was thirsty, and ye gave me drink: I was a stranger, and ye took me in: 36 naked, and ye clothed me: I was sick, and ye visited me: I was in prison, and ye came unto me.

Jesus lists some of the acts of compassion the sheep performed. The need for compassion still exists today, and many people feed the hungry, satisfy the thirsty, house the homeless, clothe the destitute, and visit the sick and imprisoned. In all of these actions Jesus said they encountered Him.

LESSON 11 • FEBRUARY 9, 2025

37 Then shall the righteous answer him, saying, Lord, when saw we thee an hungered, and fed thee? or thirsty, and gave thee drink? 38 When saw we thee a stranger, and took thee in? or naked, and clothed thee? 39 Or when saw we thee sick, or in prison, and came unto thee?

Few people have seen Jesus with unmistakable certainty. Though possible, it is a bit unlikely that anyone living today has had a face-toface encounter with the Savior. Conversely, we may have seen Christ in others or recognized an opportunity to serve Him by ministering to others.

Here the righteous ask the King some questions. According to what they knew about Christ, He was never hungry, thirsty, a stranger, naked, sick, or imprisoned, and as a result they were confused. Evidently, they sacrificed themselves to attend to someone else, and their charity pleased God.

40 And the King shall answer and say unto them, Verily I say unto you, Inasmuch as ye have done it unto one of the least of these my brethren, ye have done it unto me.

Jesus calms the sheep by referring them to their merciful deeds born of God's love for them. The brethren of Christ were not only His siblings; they included all people who inhabited the land and shared a bond with Christ through His sufferings and afflictions. Jesus stresses the "least" of His brethren, highlighting the humility exercised by the righteous in serving those thought unworthy of service. He then identifies with those people, making their pain, sorrow, and tribulation His own.

QUESTION 1
What does Christ promise those who are at His right hand (**Matthew 25:34**)?

III. THE CURSED (vv. 41–45)

In contrast to the blessed, those on the left are marked for destruction. Instead of being commended by the King, they are rejected. Their sin is one of inaction. Their failure to provide for the needs of others served as a reflection of their lack of faith in God, and love for Him and His people. They are assigned a place along with the devil, known for his selfish and evil ways. Their unrighteous acts (or lack of righteous acts) reflect a disregard for others (much like Satan). In the end, they will find themselves cast into eternal punishment.

Judgment and Punishment (verses 41–45)

41 Then shall he say also unto them on the left hand, Depart from me, ye cursed, into everlasting fire, prepared for the devil and his angels: 42 for I was an hungered, and ye gave me no meat: I was thirsty, and ye gave me no drink: 43 I was a stranger, and ye took me not in: naked, and ye clothed me not: sick, and in prison, and ye visited me not.

The Lord uses the same standards for both groups and parallels them to each other. Whereas Jesus invited those on the right to come, He commands those on the left to depart. Because the goats chose not to serve those in need, they were condemned to death. Just as God made the kingdom of heaven ready for the righteous, He made the everlasting fire ready for the unrighteous (**Revelation 20:11–15**).

LESSON 11 • FEBRUARY 9, 2025

Originally the everlasting fire was designated for Satan and his followers. But since the entrance of sin into the world and the introduction of death by sin, man was destined to join Satan in this inferno. God did not prepare this place for mankind because He is "not willing that any should perish" (**2 Peter 3:9**). But since God is just, man's disobedience demanded that he be punished unless he made proper atonement. Christ made that atonement, so man must live through the One who paid his debt. Otherwise, he must suffer God's judgment.

44 Then shall they also answer him, saying, Lord, when saw we thee an hungered, or athirst, or a stranger, or naked, or sick, or in prison, and did not minister unto thee? 45 Then shall he answer them, saying, Verily I say unto you, Inasmuch as ye did it not to one of the least of these, ye did it not to me.

The goats' reply echoes the sheep's, but there may be a difference in the tone. While the sheep may have been pleasantly surprised by Jesus' report, the goats were desperately shocked by His convicting words. They pleaded hopelessly after hearing their sentence, but the King had rendered His ruling. This contrast brings another issue to the surface. Neither the sheep nor the goats appear puzzled by their destination, but they seem bewildered by the reason for going there. None of them expected to live or die based on how they treated Jesus because no one believed they ever had the opportunity.

QUESTION 2
In contrast, what does He promise those on His left (**v. 41**)?

BIBLE APPLICATION

AIM: Students will understand God's commitment to the poor.

Our society is keen on assigning places of honor based on certain criteria—looks, money, popularity, charisma, etc. As a result, those who are without these things often get overlooked. This is true even for believers. It is easier to serve those who we feel deserve our help—starving children in Third World countries or our friends, for example. However, we often ignore and make assumptions about the homeless man we see daily. It is important to note that Christ did not "fit in" with His community. He was not attractive (**Isaiah 53:2**), did not have money (**Luke 8:1–3**), and was homeless (**Matthew 8:20**). When we choose to serve "the least," we are often choosing to serve those who may be in similar situations as Christ when He walked the earth.

STUDENTS' RESPONSES

AIM: Students will participate in God's commitment to the poor through service and compassion.

We are often faced with opportunities to serve those who are less fortunate than we are. Our care for those in need is a reflection of our heart and relationship with Christ. Christ is serious about this reality and teaches that there are places of eternal honor and eternal punishment reserved. Pray that God shows you ways to serve others. Be open to His challenging you to think out of the box and beyond your comfort zone. It could be serving the homeless in your community, traveling to serve people in a different country, fostering or adopting a child, or caring for a missionary. However He leads, remember His words that whatever you do to the least of these, you do to Him.

LESSON 11 • FEBRUARY 9, 2025

PRAYER

Jesus, as we serve and care for others, may we always give from our hearts. In Jesus' Name we pray. Amen.

DIG A LITTLE DEEPER

The Parable of the Sheep and the Goats Matthew 25:31-46

The "Parable of the Sheep and the Goats" reveals profound truths that are often overlooked but significant for believers. It challenges us to live out God's values and expectations in a tangible and life-changing way. Jesus paints a vivid picture of Himself separating people into two groups, akin to a shepherd distinguishing between sheep and goats. The criteria for this separation is rooted in how they treated the least among them—the hungry, thirsty, stranger, naked, sick, and imprisoned. Those who extended care and compassion to the vulnerable are placed on the right, signifying their righteousness and the promise of eternal life. Conversely, those who neglected the needs of the least are positioned on the left, signifying their condemnation.

The profound significance of serving the least underscores the core principles of compassion, love, and empathy for those who are suffering and in need. It echoes Jesus' teaching that the second greatest commandment is to "love your neighbor as yourself." Moreover, Jesus identifies Himself with the least of society, emphasizing that when we serve them, we are serving Christ Himself.

This parable unveils that God's kingdom is built upon the pillars of justice, mercy, and care for the marginalized. Those who actively engage in serving the least demonstrate their alignment with these divine values. Beyond mere belief, this parable becomes a litmus test for genuine faith and discipleship. We are challenged to move beyond words and are compelled to translate our faith into action by extending our hands to help those in need.

HOW TO SAY IT

Recipient.   ri-**CIP**-ee-ent.

DAILY HOME BIBLE READINGS

MONDAY
You Must Be Ready
(Matthew 24:37–44)

TUESDAY
Compassion and Justice for the Poor
(Leviticus 19:9–15)

WEDNESDAY
Open Your Hand to the Poor
(Deuteronomy 15:7–11)

THURSDAY
Celebrate with Presents for the Poor
(Esther 9:19–23)

FRIDAY
Do Not Forget the Oppressed
(Psalm 10:12–18)

SATURDAY
Share Resources with the Poor
(Romans 15:22–28)

SUNDAY
Minister to the Least
(Matthew 25:31–46)

PREPARE FOR NEXT SUNDAY

Read **Ephesians 6:10–20** and study "Clothed and Ready."

LESSON 11 • FEBRUARY 9, 2025

Sources:

Hebrew-Greek Key Word Study Bible, King James Version. Chattanooga, TN: AMG Publishers, Inc., 1991.

Keener, Craig S. *The IVP Bible Background Commentary: New Testament.* Downers Grove, IL: Intervarsity Press, 1993. 118–119.

Radmacher, Earl D., ed. *Nelson Study Bible, New King James Version.* Nashville, TN: Thomas Nelson Publishers, 1997. 1620–1625.

Ryrie, Charles C. *Ryrie Study Bible, New International Version.* Chicago, IL: Moody Press, 1986. 1358.

Unger, Merrill F. *The New Unger's Bible Dictionary.* Chicago, IL: Moody Press, 1988. 72, 940–994, 1211.

Walvoord, John F., and Roy B. Zuck, eds. *The Bible Knowledge Commentary: New Testament.* Wheaton, IL: Victor Books, SP Publications, Inc., 1983. 80–81.

COMMENTS / NOTES:

LESSON 12 • FEBRUARY 16, 2025

CLOTHED AND READY

BIBLE BASIS: EPHESIANS 6:10–20

BIBLE TRUTH: Christians can better serve God as they fortify themselves with truth, righteousness, peace, faith, salvation, the Word of God, and prayer.

MEMORY VERSE: "Put on the whole armour of God, that ye may be able to stand against the wiles of the devil" (Ephesians 6:11).

LESSON AIM: By the end of the lesson, your students will: EXAMINE the epistle's teaching to put on the whole armor of God; VALUE the feeling of being prepared to serve God; and ARM themselves with those character traits needed to best serve God.

BACKGROUND SCRIPTURE: Ephesians 6:10–20; Colossians 3:12–17—Read and incorporate the insights gained from the Background Scriptures into your study of the lesson.

LESSON SCRIPTURE

EPHESIANS 6:10–20, KJV

10 Finally, my brethren, be strong in the Lord, and in the power of his might.

11 Put on the whole armour of God, that ye may be able to stand against the wiles of the devil.

12 For we wrestle not against flesh and blood, but against principalities, against powers, against the rulers of the darkness of this world, against spiritual wickedness in high places.

13 Wherefore take unto you the whole armour of God, that ye may be able to withstand in the evil day, and having done all, to stand.

14 Stand therefore, having your loins girt about with truth, and having on the breastplate of righteousness;

15 And your feet shod with the preparation of the gospel of peace;

16 Above all, taking the shield of faith, wherewith ye shall be able to quench all the fiery darts of the wicked.

17 And take the helmet of salvation, and the sword of the Spirit, which is the word of God:

18 Praying always with all prayer and supplication in the Spirit, and watching thereunto with all perseverance and supplication for all saints;

19 And for me, that utterance may be given unto me, that I may open my mouth boldly, to make known the mystery of the gospel,

20 For which I am an ambassador in bonds: that therein I may speak boldly, as I ought to speak.

BIBLICAL DEFINITIONS

A. Wiles (Ephesians 6:11) *methodeia* (Gk.)—Cunning arts, deceit, craft, trickery.

B. Withstand (v. 13) *anthistemi* (Gk.)—To set one's self against, to withstand, oppose.

LESSON 12 • FEBRUARY 16, 2025

LIFE NEED FOR TODAY'S LESSON

AIM: Students will know that proper preparation can give assurance that certain things are accomplished.

INTRODUCTION

A Spiritual Battle

Ephesians is unique among the epistles, as it does not explicitly address a particular problem or concern in the church of Ephesus. It can best described as a model for what the church is supposed to be. In Ephesians, Paul has written a treatise defining what it means to be the church. He communicates to them that they are recipients of every spiritual blessing in Jesus Christ. They are saved by God's grace and mandated to practice good works and walk in a manner worthy of the calling they have received. Paul then proceeds to let them know how to live as the church. They are to exhibit morally pure lives and be filled with the Spirit. With this comes the ability to walk wisely and use their time for godly purposes. They are to mutually submit to one another, and this submission encompasses their home and work life. Paul then concludes his letter with an exhortation to battle. The church is now described in a military perspective. Paul exhorts the Ephesian believers to be strong in the Lord and to put on the whole armor of God. He lets them know that they have a spiritual enemy who is out to destroy them. Then he proceeds to list the pieces of armor they will need in this battle.

BIBLE LEARNING

AIM: Students will affirm that they are divinely armed in their struggle against spiritual forces of evil.

I. THE CALL TO ARMS (Ephesians 6:10–13)

Paul exhorts the Ephesian believers to be strong in the Lord and in His power. He gives them this exhortation for two reasons. The first is that with all the things he said they have been blessed with and all the duties they have been given, Satan will most definitely want to destroy them. Therefore, they need to be plugged into God's mighty power. The second reason is that they are not fighting a physical fight. Paul says that they do not wrestle against flesh and blood but against a hierarchy of evil spiritual forces.

Be Strong in the Lord (verses 10–13)

10 Finally, my brethren, be strong in the Lord, and in the power of his might. 11 Put on the whole armor of God, that ye may be able to stand against the wiles of the devil.

Paul begins by addressing his readers as "my brethren," which emphasizes the bond and intimate relationship that exists between him and the Ephesian church. It also calls for their serious attention and intensifies the importance of the subject matter. He urges them to be strong (Gk. *endunamoo*, **en-doo-nahMAH-oh**, to empower, to increase in strength) in the Lord and in the power (Gk. *kratos*, **KRAH-tos**, vigor or strength) of His might (Gk. *ischuos*, **iss-KHOO-os**, ability, power, or strength). Using these synonyms, Paul calls on the church to rely totally on the Lord for the strength and ability to face the onslaught of the enemy that surrounds them.

Jesus told His disciples that without Him, they could do nothing (**John 15:1–5**), but Paul writes, "I can do all things through Christ which strengtheneth me" (**Philippians 4:13**; cf. **2 Corinthians 12:9–10; 1 Timothy 1:12**). We must totally rely on God's strength and power because He is all-powerful and His might is infinite, as evidenced in creation and in history. By His power and strength, God not only created the heavens and the earth, but He caused the Red Sea and the Jordan River to be driven back, the moon to stand still, the mountains to tremble, and the rocks to melt. He raised Christ from the dead (**Ephesians 1:20**) and made alive those who were dead in trespasses and sins (**2:1**). In view of these and other deeds which reveal God's omnipotence in history, Paul exhorts believers to hold fast in the Lord, the one who "is able to do exceeding abundantly above all that we ask or think, according to the power that worketh in us" (**3:20**).

Although we rely totally on the strength and might of God, we must equip ourselves with the whole armor (Gk. *panoplia*, **pan-op-LEEa**, full, total, or complete armor) of God, that ye may be able to stand against the wiles of the devil. We must recall at this point that Paul is writing from prison in Rome and probably guarded by a well-dressed and completely equipped soldier or soldiers. He has a complete picture and image of a soldier in military regalia and readiness for battle. He, therefore, writes to the brethren in Ephesus, and indeed Christians of all times, to be completely dressed and ready for battle. However, the Christian's armor is not like the Roman's, which is physical—it is God's armor, which is spiritual. It is this type of military regalia we use to withstand and overcome the wiles or craftiness of the devil.

There are a few things to learn here about the devil. First, it is a fact that demons, evil spirits, Satan, devils, or whatever name given them exist contrary to the belief of many today who say that evil spirits are a myth. However, we must be careful not to give the devil a place he does not deserve by attributing to him everything adverse that happens. We must not be afraid of him. This often leads to the worship of Satan and his agents. We must acknowledge their existence as Paul did, but we are not to be afraid of them or pay them homage.

Second, we must acknowledge that Satan, the devil, is cunning and crafty, full of fury, and prowls around like a roaring lion looking for someone to devour (**1 Peter 5:8**, NIV). Having been cast out of heaven, he is full of fury and envy. His hatred is against God, His people, and all they stand for. He has a well-organized army and is out to destroy God's kingdom and to bring with him as many people as possible into hell. Satan's craftiness can be seen throughout Scripture. He mixes falsehood with some truth to make it plausible (**Genesis 3:4, 5, 22**); quotes Scripture out of context (**Matthew 4:6**); and masquerades as an angel of light (**2 Corinthians 11:14**). Therefore, we must be properly equipped to fight him, not with human armor but God's, Paul says. The call here is urgent.

12 For we wrestle not against flesh and blood, but against principalities, against powers, against the rulers of the darkness of this world, against spiritual wickedness in high places. 13 Wherefore take unto you the whole armor of God, that ye may be able to withstand in the evil day, and having done all, to stand.

After Paul establishes the fact of the devil's existence and power and urges his audience to be fully equipped with God's own armor, Paul now gives them the reason they should be so equipped: we are not fighting against "flesh and blood," i.e., against mere, frail humans (**Galatians 1:16**), with all their physical and mental weakness (**Matthew 16:17; 1 Corinthians 15:50**). Rather, we are fighting against all types of forces in all realms of life. However, the enemy knows how to use humans to do his work, so we are often deceived into thinking that the fight is against another human being.

Paul categorizes these forces as "principalities and powers" (Gk. Gk. *arche*, **ar-KHAY**, realm, principality; *exousia*, **eks-oo-SEE-ah**, authorities; cf. **Ephesians 1:21**), as the "rulers of the darkness of this world," which speaks of those who are in tyrannical control of the world of ignorance and sin. We are also fighting against spiritual forces of "wickedness in high places" (Gk. *epouranios*, **ep-oo-RAH-nee-os**, heavenly places). Heavenly places here is the same word and therefore the same realm where Christ is enthroned at God's right hand and therefore has a special position and power above all others inhabiting this realm (**1:20**). It is also where the redeemed are seated with Him (**2:6**) as well as the home of the obedient angels (**3:10**). It is the region above the earth but below the heaven, referred to as the "domain of the air" (**2:2**).

Paul, in effect, says that since we are contending against an innumerable host of spiritual forces, we must be fully equipped and put on the full armor of God (**v. 11**). Paul repeats this call in **verse 13**. The repetition of this call intensifies its urgency. The word "wrestle" used in **verse 12** can be misleading; since wrestling is viewed as a sport, it therefore can erroneously minimize the magnitude of the battle that is facing the Christian.

The explanation is probably that the battle is so intense and violent that it is like hand-to-hand combat. It is only with such divine armament that we would "be able to withstand in the evil day," that is, in the day of severe trial and temptation and onslaught of the evil one (cf. **Psalm 49:5**). The implication here is that we must always be ready and on guard since we do not know when these crises will occur.

QUESTION 1

Whom does Paul identify as the believers' opponent in battle (**Ephesians 6:12**)?

II. THE SOLDIER'S ARMOR (vv. 14–17)

Next Paul describes the armor of God. This armor resembles the armor of a Roman soldier. It consists of a belt, breastplate sandals, shield, helmet, and sword. Paul describes these items as the virtues the Christian must put on in the fight against their spiritual adversaries. The equipment is listed in the exact order the Roman soldier would put them on. The first piece of armor is the belt of truth. The next piece of armor is the breastplate of righteousness. After the breastplate is the footgear, the readiness of the Gospel of peace.

Spiritual Armor (verses 14–17)

14 Stand therefore, having your loins girt about with truth, and having on the breastplate of righteousness;

To "stand," here and in verse 11, does not imply passivity, where a soldier is pictured standing like a brick wall waiting for Satan's attack. Rather, Paul paints a picture of a soldier equipped and drawn up in battle array, rushing into war making full use of God's weapons of war for attacks and defense. It is then that the soldier would be able to stand his ground and resist the evil one, and the devil will flee from him (**James 4:7**; cf. **Matthew 10:22**). The picture is that of a soldier who is alert, vigilant, one that is never asleep and never taken unaware by the devil, who cunningly likes to attack at odd times. This is the picture of the

LESSON 12 • FEBRUARY 16, 2025

Christian Paul paints here, a strong and stable Christian who remains firm against the wiles of the devil (**v. 11**), even in a time of crisis or pressure.

In the next five verses, Paul details the six major pieces of the soldier's armor and gives the function of each one of them: the belt, the breastplate, the boots, the shield, the helmet, and the sword. They represent truth, righteousness, the Gospel of peace, faith, salvation, and the Word of God, respectively. All these pieces of spiritual armor equip us to battle against the evil powers.

The first piece of equipment which Paul lists is the belt of truth: "having your loins girt about with truth." The belt or the girdle, usually made of leather, is tied around the waist and used to brace the armor tight against the body. As the soldier buckles the belt, he feels a sense of hidden strength and confidence. One can see this watching people prepare to fight. One of the first things the fighters can do is take off their hair scarf or neck piece, tie it around their waist, and confidently beckon the other for a fight. As he or she waits for the other person to make a move, one could sense his or her feeling of confidence and inner strength. The belt is also used to hold daggers, swords, and other weapons to give the soldier freedom of movement when marching.

Paul says that the Christian's belt is truth. The two possible types of truth meant here are (1) the truth, as God's revelation in Christ and the Scripture, and (2) truth, as in honesty or integrity. Only the truth can dispel the devil's lies and set us free (**John 8:31–36, 43–45**). The psalmist says that God requires truth in the inward being (**Psalm 51:6**), and Paul says that we are to speak the truth in love (**Ephesians 4:15**). A common piece of advice is that if you speak the truth the first time, you will not worry to find another lie in future. Truth will always prevail, and lies and dishonesty will always be exposed. Honesty and integrity are marks of bravery, but lies are a sign of cowardice. The opposite of truth is lies, and the Bible says that Satan is the father of lies (**John 8:44**, NIV). Therefore we cannot beat him at his own game. Truth is the only thing that will dispel him, because he hates truth.

The second piece of the Christian's weaponry Paul mentions here is the breastplate (Gk. *thorax*, **THO-raks**) of righteousness. A breastplate is described as the armor that covers the body from neck to the thighs, the vital parts of the body. It consists of two parts, one for the back and the other for the front. Here, Paul says that the equipment for protection is righteousness (Gk. *dikaiosune*, **dee-keye-o-SOO-neigh**), which is often translated in Pauline epistles as "justification." This is theologically explained as the process whereby God through Christ puts the sinner in a right relationship with Himself. The most amazing gift for unjust sinners is to stand before the almighty, just God and not to be condemned, but accepted and clothed with God's righteousness through Christ as if they had not sinned. It is the believer's assurance that through Christ, all of our sins are forgiven and the barrier between God and us has been removed (**Isaiah 59:1–2**). This is the work of grace, which God wrought through the death of His Son Jesus on the Cross.

One of Satan's greatest weapons is slander, to accuse us through our conscience. Therefore, there is no greater defensive weapon for the Christian against the slanderous attack of the devil than the assurance of a right relationship with the Father through His Son (**2 Corinthians 5:21**). Paul assures the Roman believers of this fact: "There is therefore now no condemnation to them, which are in Christ Jesus, who walk not after the flesh, but after the

Spirit…Who shall lay any thing to the charge of God's elect? It is God that justifieth. Who is he that condemneth? It is Christ that died, yea rather, that is risen again, who is even at the right hand of God, who also maketh intercession for us" (**Romans 8:1, 33–34**). This relationship disarms the devil and offers protection for the Christian.

To successfully ward off the devil's unceasing slanderous attack, we must maintain that relationship with the Father by using the weapons of righteousness for the right hand and for the left (**2 Corinthians 6:7**). The righteousness referred to here, as well as in **Ephesians 4:24 and 5:9**, is a moral righteousness. Just as the Christian is to cultivate truth to overcome the deceptions of the devil, he also has to cultivate righteousness (i.e., moral integrity) in order to overcome the devil's slanderous attacks. Without integrity and a clear conscience, one cannot defend oneself against the accusations of the devil, who accuses the brethren night and day (**Revelation 12:10**).

15 And your feet shod with the preparation of the gospel of peace;

The next weapon in the apostle's list for warfare is the boot: the preparation of the Gospel of peace. The word translated "preparation" is the Greek word *hetoimasia* (**heh-toy-mah-SEE-ah**), which means "readiness, the act of preparedness." Paul says that the Christian should put on the Gospel of peace as his army boots. Boots protect soldiers from slipping, and from thorns or objects that can pierce through their feet and thereby hinder them from marching forward into battle. The Gospel (Good News) of peace is the protective mechanism by which we are shielded from the dangerous gimmicks the devil lays in our path to hinder our walk with the Lord. The more we are ready and prepared to testify about or confess Christ to others, the better we are protected from backsliding and falling into Satan's traps and temptation. This verse is also an allusion to the prophet Isaiah's proclamation, "How beautiful upon the mountains are the feet of him that bringeth good tidings, that publisheth peace" (from **Isaiah 52:7**, cf. **Romans 10:15**). The devil hates the Gospel (Good News) of Jesus Christ, because it is the power of God and salvation to everyone that believes (**Romans 1:16**).

Boots are a vital part of a soldier's armor, and with them securely strapped on, the soldier feels a certain amount of confidence and is ready for action. Without boots, the soldier will be ill-equipped and unprepared for battle.

16 Above all, taking the shield of faith, wherewith ye shall be able to quench all the fiery darts of the wicked.

The fourth weapon is the shield of faith, which we must take above all (Gk. *en pasin*, **en PA-sin**) in the sense that it is an indispensable part of the whole armor, rather than the most important part. The phrase can be rendered: "along with or besides all these, take also the shield of faith." The Greek word here, *thureos* (**thoo-reh-OCE**), was a large oblong, four-cornered shield, which covered the whole body, rather than the small round one that covered only a smaller part of the body. The thureos is specially designed to ward off all types of dangerous darts or missiles thrown, such as the arrows, javelins, spears, or stones that were used then.

The fiery darts also probably refer to the combustible arrowheads that set fire to the enemy's fortifications, boats, houses, or wooden shields. In order to quench the fiery darts, the shields are covered with metals. What are the fiery darts of the devil as they relate to the Christian warfare? They no doubt include the following: evil thoughts, lusts, false guilt, sinful passions, temptation of various kinds, doubts, disobedience, rebellion, malice, and fear (cf. **1 Corinthians 10:13–14; 2 Corinthians 10:4–6; James 1:13–15**, etc.). The devil ceaselessly launches all these deadly, fire-tipped darts at us daily in different forms and combinations. There is one weapon to quench or extinguish them: the shield of faith. **Proverbs 30:5** says that God is a shield to them that put their trust in Him. Faith here is reliance in and taking hold of the promises of God in the work Christ fulfilled on the Cross (**1:20–22**). In times of temptation, doubts, and depression, faith is claiming the power of God (**Philippians 4:13**). With faith, we can move mountains, Jesus told His disciples (**Matthew 17:20; Luke 17:6**).

17 And take the helmet of salvation, and the sword of the Spirit, which is the word of God:

Paul adds two more pieces of warfare equipment to the list: the helmet of salvation and the sword of the Spirit. We are to take these as weapons to fight the wicked one. Paul calls the helmet "the hope of salvation" in **1 Thessalonians 5:8**, while here it is the "helmet of salvation." There seems to be no apparent difference in these passages, since salvation is both a present and a future reality. Hence, salvation is anchored in hope. This metaphor is used in the Old Testament, where the Lord wears the helmet of salvation on His head as He goes to vindicate His people, who had been oppressed (**Isaiah 59:17**). Therefore, just as soldiers receive a helmet from their army superiors in charge of supplies, Paul says we are to take (Gk. *dechomai*, **DE-kho-meye**, to receive or accept) salvation through faith as a gift from God (**2:8**). The ancient helmets were cast from iron and brass (**1 Samuel 17:5, 38**) and they offered protection for the head like the breastplate provided for the heart. Salvation is also a protective (defensive) gear that assures the Christian in both the present and the future during times of crisis and persecutions. The assurance of God's salvation, which He has wrought through Christ in us, strengthens and carries the Christian to go on fighting without giving up, even in very difficult situations. It is the confidence that what God has begun in him, He will surely bring to completion (**Philippians 1:6**; cf. **Psalm 138:8**).

The final weapon that Paul urges the Christian to take is the sword of the Spirit. While all the other five listed are primarily weapons for defense or protection, the sword is the only weapon which can clearly be used for both offense and defense. The word translated "sword" is the Greek word *machaira* (**MA-kheye-rah**), which specifically refers to a small or short sword as opposed to a large or long one. Therefore, the combat envisaged here is in close quarters. The Christian's weapon of offense is the sword of the Spirit (or "spiritual sword"), which Paul identifies immediately as the Word (Gk. *rhema*, **RAY-ma**, the spoken word) of God. Jesus foreshadowed the importance of the Spirit's words when He promised His disciples that He would fill their lips with words through the Spirit when they are brought before magistrates (**Matthew 10:17–20**).

The Bible says that the Word of God is powerful and sharper than a double-edged sword (**Hebrew 4:12**), and so we ought to use it with confidence. The Word of God refers to both the written Word (the Scripture) inspired by the Holy Spirit (**2 Timothy 3:16; 2 Peter 1:21**) and the spoken word (*rhema*), the confession and testimony which will stand forever (**Isaiah 40:8**). Jesus applied the Word to fight Satan's temptations in the wilderness of Judea (**Luke 4:1–13**). John records the victory of the saints against Satan, saying, "And they overcame him by the blood of the Lamb, and by the word of their testimony" (from **Revelation 12:11**).

The Word of God is the greatest weapon with which we can fight the devil and his gimmicks. It is amazing what victory we can have when we apply the Word of God. Through it, we dispel doubts, fears, and guilt; by it Satan is put to flight, and assurance of salvation is secured in our hearts.

The complete armor of God is made available to every Christian: truth as the girdle, righteousness as the breastplate, the Gospel as the boots, faith as the shield, salvation as the helmet, and the Word of God as the Spirit's sword (or the spiritual sword). Since the battle is not against humans, but spirits, we need all the specified weapons without leaving any out, so that we can withstand and stand firm against Satan's ceaseless onslaught against us. We must be fully equipped, always ready for battle.

QUESTION 2
What is the purpose of taking up the shield of faith (**v. 16**)?

III. THE CALL TO PRAYER (vv. 18–20)

The secret weapon of prayer is the last piece of the Christian's equipment for battle. Paul exhorts them to use all kinds of prayers in the battle against the spiritual forces of darkness. This praying and supplication is to be done "in the Spirit"; that is, these prayers should be motivated and directed by the Spirit of God, not selfish and man-centered ramblings. These prayers also are to be directed toward all the saints. We are called not only to look after ourselves but to stand with all of our brothers and sisters in Christ. We see here that our secret weapon consists of all kinds of prayers, being prayed in the Spirit, for all the saints.

Paul's Prayer Request (verses 18–20)

18 Praying always with all prayer and supplication in the Spirit, and watching thereunto with all perseverance and supplication for all saints; 19 And for me, that utterance may be given unto me, that I may open my mouth boldly, to make known the mystery of the gospel, 20 For which I am an ambassador in bonds: that therein I may speak boldly, as I ought to speak.

After listing all the armor the Christian should put in use to fight against the wiles and wickedness of the devil, Paul explains how to use them by praying. Prayer and the Word are the two most important aspects of Christian living. Without either or both of them, the Christian's life is in jeopardy, and his life may even be at the mercy of Satan and his agents. No soldier of Christ can do anything on his or her own power without seeking strength and blessing from God, the all-powerful Father, even though he or she may have all their weapons. As a believer puts each piece of the armor on and makes use of it, he or she must rely on God through prayer. Hence, Paul says, put on the whole armor while praying and watching (**vv. 18–20**). Prayer is not a one-time exercise, but should be done always (at all times), that is, constantly or habitually with all variety of prayers being "all prayer and supplication." The phrase "all prayer" (Gk. *pas*, **PAS**, prayer; proseuche, **prosew-KHEE**, prayer) probably includes both public and private, church and family prayer. It will consist of supplication (Gk. *deesis*, **deeAY-sis**), i.e., making a special request or seeking favor for some special necessity from God. It speaks of being specific instead of general in prayer. It should be done at all times, as we have already intimated, and it should be done through the Holy Spirit, who makes intercession for us even when we do not know how or what to pray (**Romans 8:26–27, 34**).

Paul calls on us to be alert (Gk. *agrupneo*, **ahgroop-NEH-o**, to watch, be attentive) as we pray and with perseverance (Gk. *proskarteresis*, **proskar-TEH-ray-sis**) as we make supplication for the saints. This means we must be persistent and resolute in our prayer, not only for ourselves, but also for all members of the family of God in which we now belong. We shall not only be alert and watchful of Satan's strategies; we should be alert to know or be aware of the needs of others so that we can pray objectively, instead of rambling away without tangible things to pray for as we intercede for others.

Paul now, for the first time in the entire letter, makes a request for himself. He asks that when prayer is made on behalf of all the saints, they should remember him in a special way in their prayers. His two-fold request is clear, simple, and noble. First, he asks that God might give him the utterance (*logos*, i.e., the word) or the correct message when he opens his mouth to speak (**Matthew 10:19**); and second, that God might give him the courage at all times to deliver the message in a proper manner (**Acts 4:13**). The prayer request is important to him since it is for the sake of the Gospel, he says, "for which I am an ambassador in chains" (**from v. 20, NKJV**). This echoes his request in **Colossians 4:2–3**, that he be endowed with power and boldness so that he could continue to make known the mystery of the Gospel. What is that mystery of the Gospel? That through Christ, there is full salvation for everyone who comes to Him in faith, both Jew and Gentile, and it is free. That through Christ the barrier of hostility which formerly existed between the Jews and Gentiles has now been removed and they are now one in God's new family (**Ephesians 3:3–7, 9**; cf. **Romans 16:25; Colossians 1:26; 2:2**). The Gospel is the mystery, which God through Christ made known, and Paul, though imprisoned at the time in a Roman jail, is an ambassador charged to proclaim this Good News.

BIBLE APPLICATION

AIM: Students will know that God has greater powers than the spiritual forces of evil.

The world is filled with fighting and hostility. Groups are often pitted against each other in opposition. Many lines are drawn in the sand, and we often resort to uncharitable words and even physical violence. The people of God are called to fight, but not against flesh and blood. We are engaged in a war against spiritual forces of darkness. Wherever we see opposition to God and His Gospel, we must know that it cannot be defeated by mere human methods. We must put on the full armor of God and rely on His power. It is our duty in these times to be clothed and ready.

STUDENTS' RESPONSES

AIM: Students will know that believers seek and proclaim peace.

The next time you are in a situation where your faith is being challenged or you are experiencing persecution, be sure to see the real enemy. Pray that the Lord would fill you with "the power of his might" and put on the whole armor of God. Create a checklist and examine whether you are clothed and ready with the full armor of God. If you are lacking a piece of equipment, pray that God would give it to you and share this with another Christian brother or sister who can mentor you in this area.

LESSON 12 • FEBRUARY 16, 2025

PRAYER

Dear Jesus, we want to grow in our relationship with You. As we pray, forgive, love, act justly, and live Your Word, the stronger we are standing against the devil. Help us to know You and obey Your way and Your will in our lives. In Jesus' Name we pray. Amen.

DIG A LITTLE DEEPER
The Armor of God
Ephesians 6:10-20

Ephesians 6:10-20 "offers indispensable guidance for spiritual warfare, emphasizing spiritual preparation, reliance on God, recognizing the true spiritual enemies, and the roles of prayer and gospel proclamation. However, some critical elements within this passage often go unnoticed or undervalued.

This passage underscores the reality that believers engage in a battle against unseen spiritual forces of evil. Acknowledging this spiritual dimension is essential, as it reveals the depth of life's struggles and the need for spiritual readiness and defense. Ephesians urges believers to "be strong in the Lord and in the strength of His might, yet God's power is sometimes overlooked. We are reminded to rely on God rather than our abilities.

Adversaries are common, we are reminded that human beings aren't the ultimate adversaries; it's spiritual entities—rulers, authorities, and spiritual forces of evil. Understanding this truth promotes compassion and love for fellow humans who may be unwittingly influenced by these forces.

The metaphorical "armor of God" represents different facets of spiritual preparedness and are often underestimated and taken for granted, but comprehending and applying them equips us to face life's challenges with wisdom and resilience.

The significance of prayer in spiritual warfare, as a means to communicate with God, identify the real issues, seek His guidance, protection, and strength, underscores the need for believers to continually seek God's help in all aspects of life.

Ephesians also encourages believers to boldly proclaim the gospel, even in adversity, recognizing the gospel itself is a potent weapon against the forces of darkness.

HOW TO SAY IT

Principality.   prin-ci-**PA**-li-tee.

DAILY HOME BIBLE READINGS

MONDAY
Ready with the Word
(Luke 4:1–12)

TUESDAY
The Battle Lines Drawn
(1 Samuel 17:19–30)

WEDNESDAY
Choosing the Right Equipment
(1 Samuel 17:31–39)

THURSDAY
The Battle is the Lord's
(1 Samuel 17:40–50)

FRIDAY
Put on the Lord Jesus Christ
(Romans 13:8–14)

SATURDAY
The Dress for God's Chosen Ones
(Colossians 3:12–17)

SUNDAY
The Whole Armor of God
(Ephesians 6:10–20)

LESSON 12 • FEBRUARY 16, 2025

PREPARE FOR NEXT SUNDAY

Read **2 Corinthians 8:1-14** and study "A Community Shares Its Resources

Sources:
Lincoln, Andrew T. *Word Biblical Commentary Ephesians*. Dallas, TX: Word Books, 1990.
Martin, Ralph P. *Interpretation: Ephesians, Colossians, and Philemon*. Louisville, KY: John Knox Press, 1991.

COMMENTS / NOTES:

LESSON 13 • FEBRUARY 23, 2025

A COMMUNITY SHARES ITS RESOURCES

BIBLE BASIS: 2 Corinthians 8:1–14

BIBLE TRUTH: A small community that possesses much can contribute to a larger community.

MEMORY VERSE: "Therefore, as ye abound in every thing, in faith, and utterance, and knowledge, and in all diligence, and in your love to us, see that ye abound in this grace also" (2 Corinthians 8:7).

LESSON AIM: By the end of the lesson, we will: RECALL Paul's attempt to get Christian communities to help one another when there was a need; SENSE the need to sometimes contribute to a larger cause than ourselves; and DECIDE to respond to a need in the larger faith community.

BACKGROUND SCRIPTURE: 1 Corinthians 13:1–7—Read and incorporate the insights gained from the Background Scriptures into your study of the lesson.

LESSON SCRIPTURE

2 CORINTHIANS 8:1–14, KJV

1 Moreover, brethren, we do you to wit of the grace of God bestowed on the churches of Macedonia;

2 How that in a great trial of affliction the abundance of their joy and their deep poverty abounded unto the riches of their liberality.

3 For to their power, I bear record, yea, and beyond their power they were willing of themselves;

4 Praying us with much intreaty that we would receive the gift, and take upon us the fellowship of the ministering to the saints.

5 And this they did, not as we hoped, but first gave their own selves to the Lord, and unto us by the will of God.

6 Insomuch that we desired Titus, that as he had begun, so he would also finish in you the same grace also.

7 Therefore, as ye abound in every thing, in faith, and utterance, and knowledge, and in all diligence, and in your love to us, see that ye abound in this grace also.

8 I speak not by commandment, but by occasion of the forwardness of others, and to prove the sincerity of your love.

9 For ye know the grace of our Lord Jesus Christ, that, though he was rich, yet for your sakes he became poor, that ye through his poverty might be rich.

10 And herein I give my advice: for this is expedient for you, who have begun before, not only to do, but also to be forward a year ago.

11 Now therefore perform the doing of it; that as there was a readiness to will, so there may be a performance also out of that which ye have.

12 For if there be first a willing mind, it is accepted according to that a man hath, and not according to that he hath not.

13 For I mean not that other men be eased, and ye burdened:

14 But by an equality, that now at this time your abundance may be a supply for their want, that their abundance also may be a supply for your want: that there may be equality.

LESSON 13 • FEBRUARY 23, 2025

BIBLICAL DEFINITIONS

A. Poor (v. 9) *ptocheuo* (Gk.)—To be destitute.

B. Rich (v. 9) *plouteo* (Gk.)—The spiritual enrichment of believers through Jesus' poverty.

LIFE NEED FOR TODAY'S LESSON

AIM: Students will learn that as others have been generous to us, we should repay with equal generosity.

INTRODUCTION

Participation for the Saints

Paul, who had written this letter from Macedonia, was appealing to the Corinthians to participate in the collection for the poor in Jerusalem. This letter tried to build on the success of his harsh letter (an earlier letter that is now lost). It led to forgiveness and reconciliation among the believers in Corinth. He was building upon the foundation that they had realigned themselves with him and obeyed his commands (**2 Corinthians 2:9**). Since they had been obedient to his directions before, Paul wanted the Corinthians to continue in their allegiance to him. His goal was their full participation in the collection for the saints in Jerusalem.

BIBLE LEARNING

AIM: Students will learn that we are a part of a larger community.

I. GIVE LIKE THE MACEDONIANS (2 Corinthians 8:1–5)

Paul wanted to call attention to the grace of God given to the Macedonian churches. He acquainted the Corinthians with the gifts of God given through them. The Macedonians were Christians who gave to the collection for the poor in Jerusalem. They were in the midst of affliction and poverty but joyfully responded because of the sense of favor God had bestowed upon them. The Macedonians gave sacrificially on behalf of other saints in need. They wanted to assist other believers and show their commitment as followers of Christ.

Give Like the Macedonians (verses 1–5)

1 Moreover, brethren, we do you to wit of the grace of God bestowed on the churches of Macedonia. 2 How that in a great trial of affliction the abundance of their joy and their deep poverty abounded unto the riches of their liberality. 3 For to their power, I bear record, yea, and beyond their power they were willing of themselves; 4 Praying us with much entreaty that we would receive the gift, and take upon us the fellowship of the ministering to the saints. 5 And this they did, not as we hoped, but first gave their own selves to the Lord, and unto us by the will of God.

The Greek word for "to wit" is *gnorizo* (**gno RID-zo**), which means to make known. The word for "grace" in Greek is *charis* (**KHAR ece**), which is also translated as "gift." Paul wanted to make known God's gift of grace delivered to the churches of Macedonia.

Paul said that the trials the Corinthians had gone through had become a benefit to them. The Greek word for the phrase "trial of affliction" is *dokime thlipsis* (**dok-ee-MAY THLIP-sis**), which means test of tribulation. Despite their tribulations, the Corinthians had maintained their joy. The Greek word for "liberality" is *haplotes* (**hap-LOT-ace**), which is also translated as "sincerity" or "generosity." Although the Corinthians had dealt with deep poverty, they had been rich in generosity.

The Greek word for "power" is *dunamis* (**DOOnam-is**), which means ability. The word for "bear record" in Greek is *martureo* (**mar-tooREH-o**), which means to testify. The phrase "willing of themselves" comes from the Greek word *authairetos* (**ow-THAH-ee-ret-os**), which means self-chosen or voluntary. Paul complimented the Corinthians on their willingness to serve. He testified that the Corinthians gave above and beyond what they had financially.

The Greek word for "praying" is *deomai* (**DEHom-ahee**), which means urgently pleading. *Paraklesis* (**par-AK-lay-sis**) is the Greek word for "entreaty," which is also translated as "exhortation." The Corinthians almost begged Paul to receive the gift that they were giving. The Corinthians also wanted Paul to accept the fellowship of ministering to the saints. The Greek words for "fellowship" and "ministering" are *koinonia* (**koy-nohn-EE-ah**) and *diakonia* (**dee-ak-on-EE-ah**), respectively. *Koinonia* means community, communion, or joint participation; *diakonia* means serving. The Corinthians not only wanted to continue communicating with Paul, but also continue helping Paul in any way possible.

In this verse, Paul continued to emphasize how the Corinthians had gone above and beyond expectations. The phrase "not as we hoped" actually means "beyond our hopes." The Corinthians gave themselves to God first, and then they gave their money to Paul. They even gave their money "by the will of God." The Greek word for "will" is *thelema* (**THEL-ay-mah**), which means pleasure. The Corinthians pleased God with their giving.

SEARCH THE SCRIPTURES

QUESTION 1
1a. Paul stated how God's gift of grace was given to which churches?

1b. What made the generosity of the saints in our lesson so outstanding?

II. TITUS' VISIT
(2 Corinthians 8:6–8)

Titus, who was Paul's representative, had previously encouraged the Corinthians to give toward the collection for the poor. But in light of their recent conflict with Paul, they had lost their zeal for collections (7:2–15). When affliction abounds in our lives, we should still be committed to God and to ministering to others. The Macedonians were rejoicing in the midst of their troubles; Paul was encouraging the Corinthians to do the same. He told Titus to complete the gathering of collections from the Macedonians. Paul wanted them to prove their allegiance to him and their love for others.

Give as You Promised
(verses 6–8)

6 Insomuch that we desired Titus, that as he had begun, so he would also finish in you the same grace also. 7 Therefore, as ye abound in every thing, in faith, and utterance, and knowledge, and in all diligence, and in your love to us, see that ye abound in this grace also. 8 I speak not by commandment, but by occasion of the forwardness of others, and to prove the sincerity of your love.

Titus had encouraged the Corinthian church to give in the first place. Paul hoped that Titus could encourage them to keep giving. The Greek word for "desired" is *parakaleo* (**par-ak-al-EHo**), which means to encourage or exhort. The word for "finish" in Greek is *epiteleo* (**ep-eetel-EH-o**), which is also translated as "to fulfill completely." Paul was urging Titus to encourage the Corinthians to fully complete their giving.

LESSON 13 • FEBRUARY 23, 2025

The Greek word for "abound" is *perisseuo* (**per-is-SYOO-o**), which means excel. The word for "utterance" in Greek is *logos* (**LOG-os**), which is translated as "word." *Spoude* (**spoo-DAY**) is the Greek word for "diligence"; it means earnestness. Paul said that the Corinthians had excelled in their faith, speech, knowledge of the Word, earnestness, and love for Paul and Titus. However, Paul wanted to make sure that they excelled at the grace of giving as well.

The Greek word for "commandment" is *epitage* (**ep-ee-tag-AY**), which means decree. The word for "forwardness" is *spoude* (**spoo-DAY**), which is the same word used for "diligence" in the previous verse. Paul was not making a decree that the Corinthians must give more, but he wanted them to have the chance to prove the sincerity of their love.

SEARCH THE SCRIPTURES
QUESTION 2
2a. The Corinthian church was celebrated by Paul for their many good things, and he encouraged them to _____

2b. Who was Titus and what was his purpose?

III. GIVING LIKE CHRIST
(2 Corinthians 8:9)

Jesus gave up His position and became a human. He was born in poor circumstances, lived a poor life, and died in poverty—all so He may bestow His favor upon us. "In whom we have redemption through his blood, the forgiveness of sins, according to the riches of his grace" (**Ephesians 1:7**).

Give in Response to God's Grace (Verse 9)

9 For ye know the grace of our Lord Jesus Christ, that, though he was rich, yet for your sakes he became poor, that ye through his poverty might be rich.

Paul also reminded the Corinthians of the unselfishness of Christ in order to encourage them to remain unselfish as well. Paul said the Corinthians "know the grace of our Lord Jesus Christ." The Greek word for "know" is *ginosko* (**ghin-OCE-ko**), which means to be sure of something. The word for "grace" in Greek is *charis* (**KHAR-ece**), which can be translated as "favor." Christ did the ultimate favor for the Corinthians, and all of us, by leaving His throne in Heaven as King of kings and coming down to earth in the form of a child. Despite His eternal royalty, Christ came to earth as a baby born in a manger, who grew up having to work as a carpenter. Ultimately, Christ made the ultimate sacrifice by allowing Himself to be crucified on the Cross, to accomplish salvation for all who are in Him. Christ's poverty made us rich in grace and mercy.

IV. NO BURDEN IN GIVING
(2 Corinthians 8:10–14)

Paul urged the Corinthians to complete the collections for the poor that they had planned a year earlier (**2 Corinthians 9:2**). The gifts offered should be in proportion to what they were able to give. God does not want us to be burdened by giving that which we cannot sacrifice. Whatever we give, we should do it willingly. "Every man according as he purposeth in his heart, so let him give; not grudgingly, or of necessity: for God loveth a cheerful giver" (**v. 7**).

Give According to Your Ability (verses 10–14)

10 And herein I give my advice: for this is expedient for you, who have begun before, not only to do, but also to be forward a year ago. 11 Now therefore

perform the doing of it; that as there was a readiness to will, so there may be a performance also out of that which ye have. 12 For if there be first a willing mind, it is accepted according to that a man hath, and not according to that he hath not. 13 For I mean not that other men be eased, and ye burdened: 14 But by an equality, that now at this time your abundance may be a supply for their want, that their abundance also may be a supply for your want: that there may be equality:

Paul gave the Corinthians his advice on what to do with their giving. The word for "advice" in Greek is *gnome* (**GNO-may**), which means counsel or judgment. The word "expedient" comes from the Greek word *sumphero* (**soom-FER-o**), which means profitable. The word for "be forward" in Greek is *thelo* (**THEL-o**), which means determined or willed. Paul wanted them not only to continue to give, but also to continue to be determined, just as they had been a year earlier. The Greek word for "perform" is *epiteleo* (**ep-ee-tel-EH-o**), which means to finish. Paul challenged the Corinthians to finish their giving. He said that just as there was a readiness and determination to give before (the word for "will" is the same word used for "be forward" in the previous verse), the Corinthians should be determined to finish their giving according to what they had to give.

Paul reminded the Corinthians that they could only give what they had. He emphasized the importance of the right attitude in giving. The Greek word for "willing mind" is similar to the word for "readiness" in **verse 11**. *Prothumia* (**proth-oo-MEE-ah**) is the Greek word used in this verse, and it can be translated as "forwardness of mind" or "readiness of mind." There is a definite theme of willingness to give within this text. The word for "accepted" in Greek is *euprosdektos* (**yoo-PROS-dek-tos**), which means well-received. Paul suggested that the proper attitude in giving is more important than the amount being given. He said that the gift is well-received according to what the Corinthians were able to give and not according to what they could not give.

Paul did not want to put the entire burden on the Corinthians to do all of the giving to the ministry. He also didn't want the Corinthians to give so much that they suffered from not having enough for themselves. Paul knew that others needed to give as well, but he believed there should be equality in giving. The word for "equality" in Greek is *isotes* (**ee-SOT-ace**), which means "equity." The Greek word for "want" is *husterema* (**hoos-TER-ay-mah**), which means lack. Paul said that the Corinthians should be able to meet the lack of others now so that in the future, if the Corinthians were ever in lack, others could help them. Since Christians shared supplies in times of need, this is entirely possible.

BIBLE APPLICATION

AIM: Students will understand the importance of giving generously and uniting with other churches in fellowship:

The United States is one of the wealthiest nations in the world. Our understanding of rich and poor is quite different from other nations in the world where people live on much less. We know abundance, yet our economy still suffers. The unemployment rate is high. Many churchgoers are unemployed, yet we are still challenged to give generously. Paul exhorted the Corinthian church to do just that. How might those who have the means reach out to those in your congregation who have needs?

STUDENTS' RESPONSES

AIM: Students will reflect on their personal giving over the past year:

Take some real time to consider your spending. What might it say about you? Evaluate some things you have spent money on that may be considered frivolous purchases. Think about selling some of those items and using the money to support a missions effort at a local church.

PRAYER

Father, we thank You for providing for us. We thank You for giving us so many blessings. We ask that these blessings would not stop with us but that they would flow to others who do not have as much as we have. We ask that You would give us generous hearts and willing spirits to give to those in need. In Jesus' Name we pray. Amen.

DIG A LITTLE DEEPER
2 Corinthians 8:1-14

In 2 Corinthians 8:1-14, Paul underscores the significance of generous giving, drawing lessons from the Corinthian and Macedonian churches. These teachings are pertinent to both the church and the community. Their act of giving was not out of obligation but genuine love for God. Your attitude about your gift is just as important as the gift itself. How do you give? What are your feelings and thoughts as offerings are received?

Despite facing hardships, the Macedonian churches gave generously, setting a model of selflessness. Paul encourages the Corinthians to excel in giving, emphasizing the sincerity of love through generosity. Paul emphasizes the example of Jesus, who, though rich, became poor for our sake so that we might become rich through him. This illustrates sacrificial giving and the importance of considering the needs of others above our own desires.

Paul further emphasized that it was only right and fair that everyone give from their heart and according to their capacity. Subsequently those resources should be distributed fairly to those in need to ensure that everyone's needs may be met. In the early church, there were no welfare systems. The church took care of the people. How do we measure in this regard?

Do you feel like those who are rich are obligated to support the work of the church? If you were rich, what would you feel obliged to give? We know that by giving generously, we participate in God's work, contribute to the well-being of others, and exemplify the values of compassion and selflessness taught by Jesus Christ. What have you experienced that has made you draw back in your giving?

When done correctly, giving sustains church operations, enabling community outreach, spiritual guidance, and resource provision. Generosity that extends beyond church walls aids in initiatives like poverty relief, healthcare, and disaster relief. Are you a cheerful giver?

HOW TO SAY IT

Intreaty.   in-**TREE**-tee.

LESSON 13 • FEBRUARY 23, 2025

DAILY HOME BIBLE READINGS

MONDAY
Treasure in Heaven
(Mark 10:17–27)

TUESDAY
The Measure of Your Gift
(Luke 6:34–38)

WEDNESDAY
Giving in Love
(1 Corinthians 13:1–7)

THURSDAY
Show Proof of Your Love
(2 Corinthians 8:16–24)

FRIDAY
Sowing and Reaping Bountifully
(2 Corinthians 9:1–6)

SATURDAY
God Loves a Cheerful Giver
(2 Corinthians 9:7–15)

SUNDAY
A Wealth of Generosity
(2 Corinthians 8:1–14)

PREPARE FOR NEXT SUNDAY

Read John 1:29-34 and study "The Word of God."

Sources:
Blue Letter Bible. BlueLetterBible.org. http://www.blueletterbible.org/ (accessed December 2, 2012).
Craig Evans, and Stanley Porter, ed. *Dictionary of New Testament Background*. Downers Grove, IL: IVP Academic, 2000.
Richards, Lawrence O. *The Teacher's Commentary*. Wheaton: Victor Books, 1989.

COMMENTS / NOTES:

The Symbol of the Church Of God In Christ

The Symbol of the Church Of God In Christ is an outgrowth of the Presiding Bishop's Coat of Arms, which has become quite familiar to the Church. The design of the Official Seal of the Church was created in 1973 and adopted in the General Assembly in 1981 (July Session).

The obvious GARNERED WHEAT in the center of the seal represents all of the people of the Church Of God In Christ, Inc. The ROPE of wheat that holds the shaft together represents the Founding Father of the Church, Bishop Charles Harrison Mason, who, at the call of the Lord, banded us together as a Brotherhood of Churches in the First Pentecostal General Assembly of the Church, in 1907.

The date in the seal has a two-fold purpose: first, to tell us that Bishop Mason received the baptism of the Holy Ghost in March 1907 and, second, to tell us that it was because of this outpouring that Bishop Mason was compelled to call us together in February of 1907 to organize the Church Of God In Christ.

The RAIN in the background represents the Latter Rain, or the End-time Revivals, which brought about the emergence of our Church along with other Pentecostal Holiness Bodies in the same era. The rain also serves as a challenge to the Church to keep Christ in the center of our worship and service, so that He may continue to use the Church Of God In Christ as one of the vehicles of Pentecostal Revival before the return of the Lord.

This information was reprinted from the book *So You Want to KNOW YOUR CHURCH* by Alferd Z. Hall, Jr.

COGIC AFFIRMATION OF FAITH

We believe the Bible to be the inspired and only infallible written Word of God.

We believe that there is One God, eternally existent in three Persons: God the Father, God the Son, and God the Holy Spirit.

We believe in the Blessed Hope, which is the rapture of the Church of God, which is in Christ at His return.

We believe that the only means of being cleansed from sin is through repentance and faith in the precious Blood of Jesus Christ.

We believe that regeneration by the Holy Ghost is absolutely essential for personal salvation.

We believe that the redemptive work of Christ on the Cross provides healing for the human body in answer to believing in prayer.

We believe that the baptism in the Holy Ghost, according to Acts 2:4, is given to believers who ask for it.

We believe in the sanctifying power of the Holy Spirit, by whose indwelling the Christian is enabled to live a Holy and separated life in this present world. Amen.

The Doctrines of the Church Of God In Christ

THE BIBLE

We believe that the Bible is the Word of God and contains one harmonious and sufficiently complete system of doctrine. We believe in the full inspiration of the Word of God. We hold the Word of God to be the only authority in all matters and assert that no doctrine can be true or essential if it does not find a place in this Word.

THE FATHER

We believe in God, the Father Almighty, the Author and Creator of all things. The Old Testament reveals God in diverse manners, by manifesting His nature, character, and dominions. The Gospels in the New Testament give us knowledge of God the "Father" or "My Father," showing the relationship of God to Jesus as Father, or representing Him as the Father in the Godhead, and Jesus himself that Son (St. John 15:8, 14:20). Jesus also gives God the distinction of "Fatherhood" to all believers when He explains God in the light of "Your Father in Heaven" (St. Matthew 6:8).

THE SON

We believe that Jesus Christ is the Son of God, the second person in the Godhead of the Trinity or Triune Godhead. We believe that Jesus was and is eternal in His person and nature as the Son of God who was with God in the beginning of creation (St. John 1:1). We believe that Jesus Christ was born of a virgin called Mary according to the Scripture (St. Matthew 1:18), thus giving rise to our fundamental belief in the Virgin

Birth and to all of the miraculous events surrounding the phenomenon (St. Matthew 1:18–25). We believe that Jesus Christ became the "suffering servant" to man; this suffering servant came seeking to redeem man from sin and to reconcile him to God, his Father (Romans 5:10). We believe that Jesus Christ is standing now as mediator between God and man (I Timothy 2:5).

THE HOLY GHOST

We believe the Holy Ghost or Holy Spirit is the third person of the Trinity; proceeds from the Father and the Son; is of the same substance, equal to power and glory; and is together with the Father and the Son, to be believed in, obeyed, and worshiped. The Holy Ghost is a gift bestowed upon the believer for the purpose of equipping and empowering the believer, making him or her a more effective witness for service in the world. He teaches and guides one into all truth (John 16:13; Acts 1:8, 8:39).

THE BAPTISM OF THE HOLY GHOST

We believe that the Baptism of the Holy Ghost is an experience subsequent to conversion and sanctification and that tongue-speaking is the consequence of the baptism in the Holy Ghost with the manifestations of the fruit of the spirit (Galatians 5:22–23; Acts 10:46, 19:1–6). We believe that we are not baptized with the Holy Ghost in order to be saved (Acts 19:1–6; John 3:5). When one receives a baptismal Holy Ghost experience, we believe one will speak with a tongue unknown to oneself according to the sovereign will of Christ. To be filled with the Spirit means to be Spirit controlled as expressed by Paul in Ephesians 5:18,19. Since the charismatic demonstrations were necessary to help the early church to be successful in implementing the command of Christ, we, therefore, believe that a Holy Ghost experience is mandatory for all believers today.

MAN

We believe that humankind was created holy by God, composed of body, soul, and spirit. We believe that humankind, by nature, is sinful and unholy. Being born in sin, a person needs to be born again, sanctified and cleansed from all sins by the blood of Jesus. We believe that one is saved by confessing and forsaking one's sins, and believing on the Lord Jesus Christ, and that having become a child of God, by being born again and adopted into the family of God, one may, and should, claim the inheritance of the sons of God, namely the baptism of the Holy Ghost.

SIN

Sin, the Bible teaches, began in the angelic world (Ezekiel 28:11–19; Isaiah 14:12–20) and is transmitted into the blood of the human race through disobedience and deception motivated by unbelief (I Timothy 2:14). Adam's sin, committed by eating of the forbidden fruit from the tree of knowledge of good and evil, carried with it permanent pollution or depraved human nature to all his descendants. This is called "original sin." Sin can now be defined as a volitional transgression against God and a lack of conformity to the will of God. We, therefore, conclude that humankind by nature is sinful and has fallen from a glorious and righteous state from which we were created, and has become unrighteous and unholy. We therefore, must be restored to the state of holiness from which we have fallen by being born again (St. John 3:7).

SALVATION

Salvation deals with the application of the work of redemption to the sinner with restoration to divine favor and communion with God. This redemptive operation of the Holy Ghost upon sinners is brought about by repentance toward God and faith toward our Lord Jesus Christ which brings conversion, faith, justification, regeneration, sanctification, and the baptism of the Holy Ghost. Repentance is the work of God, which results in a change of mind in respect to a person's relationship to God (St. Matthew 3:1–2, 4:17; Acts 20:21). Faith is a certain conviction wrought in the heart by the Holy Spirit, as to the truth of the Gospel and a heart trust in the promises of God in Christ (Romans 1:17, 3:28; St. Matthew 9:22; Acts 26:18). Conversion is that act of God whereby He causes the regenerated sinner, in one's conscious life, to turn to Him in repentance and faith (II Kings 5:15; II Chronicles 33:12,13; St. Luke 19:8,9; Acts 8:30). Regeneration is the act of God by which the principle of the new life is implanted in humankind, the governing disposition of soul is made holy, and the first holy exercise of this new disposition is secured. Sanctification is that gracious and continuous operation of the Holy Ghost, by which He delivers the justified sinner from the pollution of sin, renews a person's whole nature in the image of God, and enables one to perform good works (Romans 6:4, 5:6; Colossians 2:12, 3:1).

ANGELS

The Bible uses the term "angel" (a heavenly body) clearly and primarily to denote messengers or ambassadors of God with such Scripture references as Revelations 4:5, which indicates their duty in heaven to praise God (Psalm 103:20), to do God's will (St. Matthew 18:10), and to behold His face. But since heaven must come down to earth, they also have a mission to earth. The Bible indicates that they accompanied God in the Creation, and also that they will accompany Christ in His return in Glory.

DEMONS

Demons denote unclean or evil spirits; they are sometimes called devils or demonic beings. They are evil spirits, belonging to the unseen or spiritual realm, embodied in human beings. The Old Testament refers to the prince of demons, sometimes called Satan (adversary) or Devil, as having power and wisdom, taking the habitation of other forms such as the serpent (Genesis 3:1). The New Testament speaks of the Devil as Tempter (St. Matthew 4:3), and it goes on to tell the works of

Satan, the Devil, and demons as combating righteousness and good in any form, proving to be an adversary to the saints. Their chief power is exercised to destroy the mission of Jesus Christ. It can well be said that the Christian Church believes in demons, Satan, and devils. We believe in their power and purpose. We believe they can be subdued and conquered as in the commandment to the believer by Jesus. "In my name they shall cast out Satan and the work of the Devil and to resist him and then he will flee (WITHDRAW) from you" (St. Mark 16:17).

THE CHURCH

The Church forms a spiritual unity of which Christ is the divine head. It is animated by one Spirit, the Spirit of Christ. It professes one faith, shares one hope, and serves one King. It is the citadel of the truth and God's agency for communicating to believers all spiritual blessings. The Church then is the object of our faith rather than of knowledge. The name of our Church, "CHURCH OF GOD IN CHRIST," is supported by I Thessalonians 2:14 and other passages in the Pauline Epistles. The word "CHURCH" or "EKKLESIA" was first applied to the Christian society by Jesus Christ in St. Matthew 16:18, the occasion being that of His benediction of Peter at Caesarea Philippi.

THE SECOND COMING OF CHRIST

We believe in the second coming of Christ; that He shall come from heaven to earth, personally, bodily, visibly (Acts 1:11; Titus 2:11–13; St. Matthew 16:27, 24:30, 25:30; Luke 21:27; John 1:14, 17; Titus 2:11); and that the Church, the bride, will be caught up to meet Him in the air (I Thessalonians 4:16–17). We admonish all who have this hope to purify themselves as He is pure.

DIVINE HEALING

The Church Of God In Christ believes in and practices Divine Healing. It is a commandment of Jesus to the Apostles (St. Mark 16:18). Jesus affirms His teachings on healing by explaining to His disciples, who were to be Apostles, that healing the afflicted is by faith (St. Luke 9:40–41). Therefore, we believe that healing by faith in God has scriptural support and ordained authority. St. James's writings in his epistle encourage Elders to pray for the sick, lay hands upon them and to anoint them with oil, and state that prayers with faith shall heal the sick and the Lord shall raise them up. Healing is still practiced widely and frequently in the Church Of God In Christ, and testimonies of healing in our Church testify to this fact.

MIRACLES

The Church Of God In Christ believes that miracles occur to convince people that the Bible is God's Word. A miracle can be defined as an extraordinary visible act of divine power, wrought by the efficient agency of the will of God, which has as its final cause the vindication of the righteousness of God's Word. We believe that the works of God, which were performed during the beginnings of Christianity, do and will occur even today where God is preached, faith in Christ is exercised, the Holy Ghost is active, and the Gospel is promulgated in the truth (Acts 5:15, 6:8, 9:40; Luke 4:36, 7:14, 15, 5:5, 6; St. Mark 14:15).

THE ORDINANCES OF THE CHURCH

It is generally admitted that for an ordinance to be valid, it must have been instituted by Christ. When we speak of ordinances of the church, we are speaking of those instituted by Christ, in which by sensible signs the grace of God in Christ and the benefits of the covenant of grace are represented, sealed, and applied to believers, and these in turn give expression to their faith and allegiance to God. The Church Of God In Christ recognizes three ordinances as having been instituted by Christ himself and, therefore, are binding upon the church practice.

THE LORD'S SUPPER (HOLY COMMUNION)

The Lord's Supper symbolizes the Lord's death and suffering for the benefit and in the place of His people. It also symbolizes the believer's participation in the crucified Christ. It represents not only the death of Christ as the object of faith, which unites the believers to Christ, but also the effect of this act as the giving of life, strength, and joy to the soul. The communicant by faith enters into a special spiritual union of one's soul with the glorified Christ.

FOOT WASHING

Foot washing is practiced and recognized as an ordinance in our Church because Christ, by His example, showed that humility characterized greatness in the kingdom of God, and that service rendered to others gave evidence that humility, motivated by love, exists. These services are held subsequent to the Lord's Supper; however, its regularity is left to the discretion of the pastor in charge.

WATER BAPTISM

We believe that Water Baptism is necessary as instructed by Christ in St. John 3:5, "UNLESS MAN BE BORN AGAIN OF WATER AND OF THE SPIRIT…"

However, we do not believe that water baptism alone is a means of salvation, but is an outward demonstration that one has already had a conversion experience and has accepted Christ as his personal Savior. As Pentecostals, we practice immersion in preference to sprinkling because immersion corresponds more closely to the death, burial, and resurrection of our Lord (Colossians 2:12). It also symbolizes regeneration and purification more than any other mode. Therefore, we practice immersion as our mode of baptism. We believe that we should use the Baptismal Formula given to us by Christ for all "…IN THE NAME OF THE FATHER, AND OF THE SON, AND OF THE HOLY GHOST…" (Matthew 28:19).

Suggested Order of Service

1. Call to order.
2. Singing.
3. Prayer.
4. **New Responsive Reading & Core Values**

ISSD: Responsive Reading

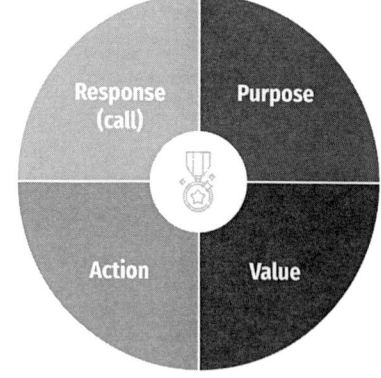

Calls for the response of worship of God
Calls for response to God (in unity)
Calls for response to God's truth

Builds identity around our core values
Builds student belief in themselves and in the mission of The Church

- To support students in achieving the curricular outcomes
- To inspire students to become engaged in comprehension and practice of scriptural commands

- For the life of The Church, it is:
  -biblical
  -historic
  -participatory
  -instructional

Suggested Order of Service

Responsive reading continued:

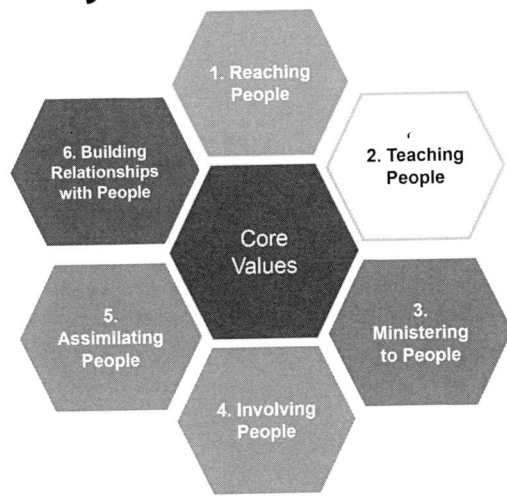

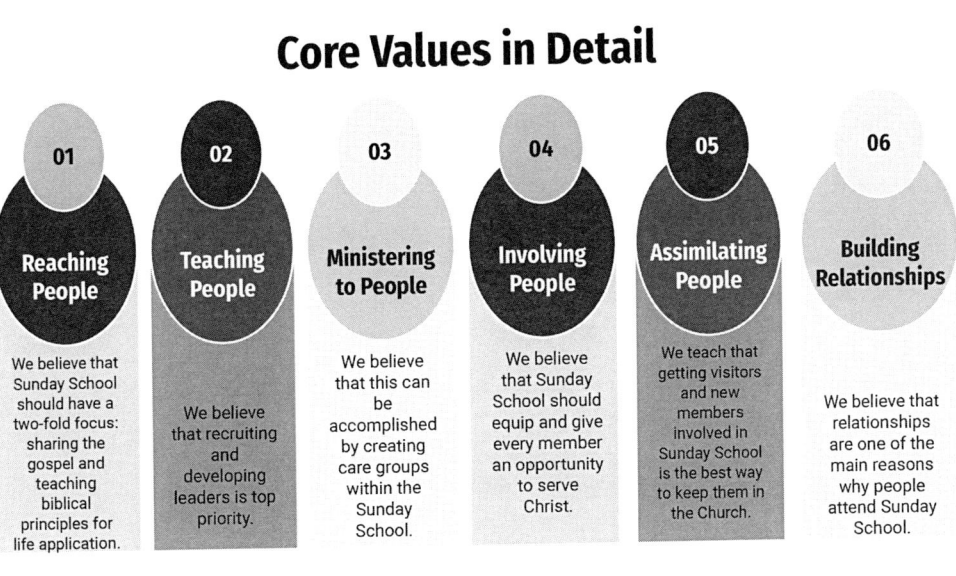

New Responsive Reading

SUPERINTENDENT/TEACHER: Behold how good and how pleasant it is for brethren to dwell together in unity! *Psalm 133:1*

SCHOOL/CLASS: But to do good and to communicate forget not: for with such sacrifices God is well pleased. *Hebrews 13:16*

SUPERINTENDENT/TEACHER: All scripture is given by inspiration of God, and is profitable for doctrine, for reproof, for correction, for instruction in righteousness. *2 Timothy 3:16*

SCHOOL/CLASS: Thy word is a lamp unto my feet, and a light unto my path. *Psalm 119:105*

SUPERINTENDENT/TEACHER: Look not every man on his own things, but every man also on the things of others. *Philippians 2:4*

SCHOOL/CLASS: He that hath a bountiful eye shall be blessed; for he giveth of his bread to the poor. *Proverbs 22:9*

SUPERINTENDENT/TEACHER: Wherefore he saith, When he ascended up on high, he led captivity captive, and gave gifts unto men. *Ephesians 4:8*

SCHOOL/CLASS: As every man hath received the gift, even so minister the same one to another, as good stewards of the manifold grace of God. *1 Peter 4:10*

SUPERINTENDENT/TEACHER: For as the body is one, and hath many members, and all the members of that one body, being many, are one body: so also is Christ. *1 Corinthians 12:12*

SCHOOL/CLASS: For as we have many members in one body, and all members have not the same office. *Romans 12:4*

SUPERINTENDENT/TEACHER: By this shall all men know that ye are my disciples, if ye have love one to another. *John 13:35*

SCHOOL/CLASS: For, brethren, ye have been called unto liberty; only use not liberty for an occasion to the flesh, but by love serve one another. *Galatians 5:13*

SUPERINTENDENT/ALL: But grow in grace, and in the knowledge of our Lord and Saviour Jesus Christ. To him be glory both now and for ever. Amen. *2 Peter 3:18*

Notes

Notes

Notes

Notes